**DIRECTIONS IN DEVELOPMENT**

# Improving Adult Literacy Outcomes

*Lessons from Cognitive Research for Developing Countries*

**DIRECTIONS IN DEVELOPMENT**

# Improving Adult Literacy Outcomes
## *Lessons from Cognitive Research for Developing Countries*

Helen Abadzi
Senior Evaluation Officer
Operations Evaluation Department

**THE WORLD BANK**
Washington, D.C.

© 2003 The International Bank for Reconstruction and Development / The World Bank
1818 H Street, NW
Washington, DC 20433
Telephone 202-473-1000
Internet www.worldbank.org
E-mail feedback@worldbank.org

All rights reserved.

1 2 3 4 05 04 03 02

The findings, interpretations, and conclusions expressed herein are those of the author(s) and do not necessarily reflect the views of the Board of Executive Directors of the World Bank or the governments they represent.

The World Bank does not guarantee the accuracy of the data included in this work. The boundaries, colors, denominations, and other information shown on any map in this work do not imply any judgment on the part of the World Bank concerning the legal status of any territory or the endorsement or acceptance of such boundaries.

**Rights and Permissions**

The material in this work is copyrighted. Copying and/or transmitting portions or all of this work without permission may be a violation of applicable law. The World Bank encourages dissemination of its work and will normally grant permission promptly.

For permission to photocopy or reprint any part of this work, please send a request with complete information to the Copyright Clearance Center, Inc., 222 Rosewood Drive, Danvers, MA 01923, USA, telephone 978-750-8400, fax 978-750-4470, www.copyright.com.

All other queries on rights and licenses, including subsidiary rights, should be addressed to the Office of the Publisher, World Bank, 1818 H Street NW, Washington, DC 20433, USA, fax 202-522-2422, e-mail pubrights@worldbank.org.

Cover photo credits: Curt Carnemark/World Bank.

**ISBN 0-8213-5493-0**

**Library of Congress Cataloging-in-Publication Data has been applied for.**

# Contents

Acknowledgments .................................................................................. vii

Acronyms and Abbreviations ................................................................ viii

Overview .................................................................................................... 1

1. Background: Adventures in Adult Literacy ..................................... 9

2. Cognitive Science in the Service of Adult Literacy ..................... 15
   *Human Evolution toward Efficient Reading* ............................................. 16
   *A Fundamental Problem: Cognitive Limitations of Unschooled*
      *People* .................................................................................................. 17
   *Skills Important for Efficient Reading* ..................................................... 22
   *Working Memory: The Reading Comprehension Bottleneck* ................... 26
   *Automaticity: Means to Overcome the Working Memory*
      *Bottleneck* ........................................................................................... 29
   *Phonological Awareness—Ability to Break Down Words* ...................... 32
   *Perceptual Learning and the Nitty-Gritty of Recognizing Letters* .......... 34
   *Beginning Readers of Various Scripts: Putting it All Together* .............. 40
   *Forgetting—Relapse into Illiteracy* .......................................................... 41
   *The Reading Difficulties of Adult Learners* ............................................ 45
   *Health Issues Affecting Reading Performance* ........................................ 47

3. Instructional and Social Issues of Literacy Acquisition ............... 61
   *Course Duration* ....................................................................................... 61
   *The Challenge of Teaching Basic Numeracy* ........................................... 62
   *Textbook Content and Time on Task for Reading* .................................. 63
   *The Challenges of Teacher Selection and Training* ................................ 64
   *Group Formation and Livelihood Training* ............................................. 66
   *Social Benefits of Adult Literacy Programs* ............................................ 68

4. **Policy Implications of Cognitive Literacy Methods** ...... 73
   *Researching Literacy Acquisition to Improve Effectiveness* ...... 74

**Annex A. Improving Reading Performance in Adult Literacy Classes of Burkina Faso** ...... 77

**Appendix. Literacy Tests and Questionnaire** ...... 93

**References** ...... 95

**Index** ...... 109

**Boxes**
Box 1. Arabic: A Very Difficult Script for Adult Learners ...... 42
Box 2. Literacy Learners May Get Limited Practice ...... 65
Box 3. REFLECT: Beneficiaries May Feel Empowered but Not Be Literate ...... 69

**Figures**
Figure 1. Example of Functional Brain Organization Differences between Literates and Illiterates ...... 19
Figure 2. The Major Processes Involved in Reading Comprehension ...... 23
Figure 3. Time Required for Reading ...... 27
Figure 4. Eye Movements and Reading Time ...... 34
Figure 5. A Forgetting Curve of Procedural Knowledge ...... 43
Figure 6. Differences in Printed and Handwritten Letters May Confuse Neoliterates ...... 49
Figure A1. Effect Sizes of Various Treatment Combinations ...... 88

# Acknowledgments

Thanks are due to the Swiss Development Cooperation, whose grant through the World Bank Consultant Trust Funds Department inspired this report and supported literacy research in Burkina Faso. Thanks are also due to Gregory Ingram, Director General, Operations Evaluation Department, and Alain Barbu, Manager, OEDST, who supported this publication.

Furthermore, I thank my World Bank colleagues Martha Ainsworth, David Klaus, and John Oxenham, as well as Profs. Richard Venezky (University of Delaware), Irving Biederman (University of Southern California, Los Angeles), Alexandra Reis (University of Algarve, Portugal), John Comings (Harvard University), and James M. Royer (University of Massachusetts) for the diligent reviews and helpful comments. Thanks are also due to Maria Pilar Barquero for processing assistance.

Finally, I would like to thank the National Literacy Institute of Burkina Faso, Organisation Suisse d' Entraide Ouvrière (OSEO), the Alpha Program of the Swiss Cooperation, the Promotion Femmes Développement Solidarité, and the Association Manegdbzanga for their help in carrying out literacy research in Burkina Faso.

Helen Abadzi
Senior Evaluation Officer
Operations Evaluation Department
April 30, 2003

# Acronyms and Abbreviations

| | |
|---|---|
| ADB | Asian Development Bank |
| AIDS | Acquired Immune Deficiency Syndrome |
| BELOISYA | Basic Education and Livelihood Opportunities for Illiterate and Semiliterate Young Adults |
| CAAS | Computer-based Academic Assessment System |
| CIDA | Canadian International Development Agency |
| DABE | Directorate of Adult Basic Education (Indonesia) |
| DIKMAS | Directorate of Adult Basic Education (Indonesia) |
| DNFE | Directorate of Non-Formal Education (Bangladesh) |
| EFA | Education for All |
| EWLP | Experimental World Literacy Programme |
| fMRI | Functional magnetic resonance imaging |
| IDA | International Development Association |
| INA | Institut National d'Alphabétisation |
| IEC | Information, education, communication |
| LIL | Learning and Innovation Loan |
| msec | milliseconds |
| NFED | Non-Formal Education Division (Ghana) |
| NORAD | Norwegian Agency for Development Cooperation |
| NGO | Nongovernmental Organization |
| OPEC | Organization of Petroleum Producing Countries |
| OSEO | Organisation Suisse d'Entraide Ouvrière |
| PRA | Participatory Rural Appraisal |
| PET | Positron Emission Tomography |
| PRSP | Poverty Reduction Strategy Plan |
| REFLECT | Regenerated Freirean Literacy Through Empowering Community Techniques |
| SDC | Swiss Agency for Development Cooperation |
| SIDA | Swedish International Development Cooperation Agency |
| UNESCO | United Nations Educational, Scientific and Cultural Organization |

## ACRONYMS AND ABBREVIATIONS

UNDP     United Nations Development Programme
UNICEF   United Nations Children's Fund
USAID    United States Agency for International Development

# Overview

Despite the existence of about one billion illiterates in the world, adult literacy programs make up 1–5 percent of government or donor budgets, and they remain severely underfunded in comparison to primary education. Though dropout and course completion rates improved in the 1990s, the outcomes of literacy instruction are still modest and may have improved little since the 1970s. The results may disappoint governments and donors who expect that once taught, people will have usable skills and remain literate. The modest results make it hard to increase coverage and to argue for increased expenditures for this sector.

The results may be due to inefficient instruction but also to the structure of human memory, which has important implications for adult literacy acquisition. The need to learn the rapid recognition of complex patterns poses problems that are not apparent to people who became expert readers in their childhood.

*Time is of essence in reading.* Reading must become automatic, fast, effortless, and accurate in order to be useful. The short-term memory (working memory) needed to store the deciphered material is exceedingly brief. In educated people it lasts about 12 seconds and holds about 7 items, and in illiterates it may even last less. If the information in short-term memory is not rehearsed or transferred to long-term memory, it gets wiped out. Neoliterates must read a word in about 1–1.5 second (45–60 words per minute) in order to understand a sentence within 12 seconds. If they take longer, they forget by the end of the sentence what they read at the beginning. This speed, which corresponds to oral-reading U.S. norms for grade 1 children, is pretty fast and not often attained in literacy classes. Research in Burkina Faso (Annex A) indicated that most literacy graduates need 2.2 seconds to read a word and are correct only 80–87 percent of the time.

The low speed and high error rate fill the valuable short-term memory with individual letters and overwhelm it. If learners read slowly, infrequently, and must make conscious decisions about letters, they read small amounts of text. Their skills will probably be lost rapidly after training, like other rarely practiced skills.

The structure of memory points towards a standard for literacy acquisition: *By the end of a literacy course, learners should read a word in about 1–1.5 seconds with about 95 percent accuracy.* At this rate, readers decipher many script features automatically. Automatic readers do not normally lapse back into illiteracy.

For reasons that are unclear, adult neoliterates may remain slow readers who read letter by letter, whereas children tend to increase reading speed and become automatic readers. Adult literacy instruction should focus on increasing speed and accuracy, objectives that are usually not central in literacy courses; literacy tests should be timed.

Efficient use of class time might help learners achieve the necessary speed and accuracy. But valuable time is often lost in oral repetition, classes may be held infrequently and attendance may be desultory. Because basic reading seems easy to teach, literacy in the developing world is often a task of poorly paid persons of limited education. Teacher selection, training, assignments, pay, classroom duration, and time on task are critical variables that determine course outcomes. Because of complexity and budget constraints, these issues may receive short shrift in planning and supervision, or they may not be carried out as expected.

People's level of education influences their ability to solve abstract problems, use readily presented data in decisions, recognize and name pictures of objects, and understand radio broadcasts. Most important, the unschooled perform less well in most memory tasks: recalling a series of digits backward and forward, remembering lists of words, reproducing a short story, reproducing complex figures that were presented, recalling common objects, remembering sequences. The limited memory and cognitive resources probably also reduce performance in literacy classes.

Empowerment has been an important expected literacy outcome. However, the available data cast some doubt on the efficacy or sustainability of empowerment as a result of literacy classes. The onetime self-reports of benefits are vulnerable to bias. Also, it is hard to understand how learners may become empowered if they do not learn to read well. Income generation ("literacy second") methods to attract and educate learners also seem to have limited outcomes. However, groups and cooperatives in West Africa have been able to acquire stable literacy skills if they study to fulfill work goals.

Research on literacy is often carried out by adult education specialists who typically lack training in cognition and neuropsychology. Thus, the many literacy departments and agencies worldwide focus on social, motivational, and methodological issues. There is limited technical understanding about enabling adults to read faster and more accurately. The instructional delivery of adult literacy could be reformulated based on state-of-the-art cognitive findings. However, more research is needed to find out which of these methods can result in sustained reading improvement and how feasible large-scale applications are. Also, more dissemination of technical information is needed among high-level decisionmakers.

What policy actions are needed to ensure that students in classes acquire fast and effortless reading? Governments and donors have strongly emphasized the management, planning, and institutional issues necessary for large-scale literacy programs to succeed. Better management is necessary but insufficient. To achieve the required high reading rates, it may be necessary for literacy programs to use more complex methods with better trained teachers and higher budgetary outlays than is currently the case. Costs per learner may increase, but costs per graduate with stable literacy skills may decrease as programs become more efficient. Governments must determine whether the increased costs of more scientifically based literacy instruction are worth the benefits and whether an increased share of education budgets for literacy instruction is justified.

## Instructional Implications

Summarized below are some principles and methods, derived from cognitive and neuropsychological research, to make literacy instruction more effective.

### *Improving the Cognitive Functions of Adult Illiterates*

Illiterates lack many neural networks of schooled people and score low in many neuropsychological tests. To remedy areas of low cognitive performance, the Neuroalfa literacy method (see details in the text) could be tried and refined. Its exercises may be broadened or shortened according to correlations with reading scores in specific languages.

Illiterate adults' working memory may be too brief for efficient reading. Literacy training may stretch it, but it may be worthwhile to give exercises for it, such as repeating increasingly longer series of digits (also part of the Neuroalfa method).

Illustrative materials used in participatory rural appraisals to help the poor articulate their community knowledge (maps, calendars, diagrams, matrices) may be useful tools in improving the visuo-spatial skills of illiterates, which are particularly poor among women.

## *Teaching Decoding of a Script*

Phonological awareness tasks should be introduced early, such as deleting the initial or final vowels or consonants, counting the number of syllables (as appropriate in various languages), or rhyming. Rather than random words, Freirean "generative" words could be used.

Instruction must help learners efficiently and quickly understand words and offer an analytical strategy for learning new letter combinations. Decoding techniques are often language- or script-specific, but many exercises have been devised, such as (a) phonographix, a system to show extensions of reading rules to similar patterns (for example, mat – cat – hat – ham – him), (b) reading pseudowords that look like real words, and (c) speed-reading letters together, though they constitute nonsense syllables.

To get the benefit of the word superiority effect, textbooks and teachers might reduce the presentation of unconnected letters and include early on the letters in words. New letters could be presented before and after words that include them (for example, paper, e, p, a, r). New texts could consist of words that have already been presented or have well-practiced letter patterns.

*Mnemonics* have been used to help learners connect letters and sounds (such as "a is for apple"). The benefits and costs are unclear. They may cause learners to make irrelevant connections rather than the instant and effortless connections that are needed between letters and sounds. On the other hand, reminders of how letters look may make the connections memorable early in a course or help readers if they start to forget after literacy training. Mnemonics may create more stable connections if learners themselves make them up according to their existing knowledge.

## *Fast Reading and Automatic Recognition of Text*

Readers must be helped to read ever faster through various technologies such as flash cards or computerized tutorials, if possible. Chanting, that is, quick turn taking with a teacher or peer establishes a rhythm and may force students to deal with larger amounts of print than they otherwise would. Same-language subtitling of films available in some parts of India for post-literacy purposes has similar effects.

Also important is repeated reading of the same text and building texts from words that are already known or have well-practiced letter sound patterns.

To bring about word automaticity, learners may *overlearn and automatize the recognition of small units.* This can be accomplished by reading a pack of cards containing small units as fast as possible over several days and recording the time required to do this. (Sheets may also be used, but learners may learn the order of the words.) This may be done once per session, and the time may be recorded every day. Over several days, the time required for the task decreases. When learners show no further improvement, they get a new list of longer words. Along with the new words, interspersed practice is given on the ones mastered earlier, to maintain old skills and build new ones.

Pairing of multiple sounds and letters can be much more effective if computerized. Computerized presentations may also engage learners and motivate them to stay and work at the tasks longer than they would otherwise do in a class. Some computerized applications may work on equipment that is cheaper than computers, such as an electronic reader and speaker by the U.S.-based Leapfrog company or the Indian-made Simputer. This and other methods may improve the reading skills of the poor if they become widely available in poorer countries.

If learners master the basics of reading within a literacy course, then vocabulary and reading comprehension must be built. This level of skills frequently is left for post-literacy courses.

## *Forgetting How to Read*

Unless learners become automatic readers by the end of a course, they may gradually forget how to read. The amount of forgetting is a function of prior exposure (in primary school, for example), practice during the literacy course, environmental opportunities to practice literacy, and innate ability.

Often, neoliterates remember the shape of letters but forget the associated sounds. Suitable mnemonics may help them keep letters and sounds connected for long-term retention.

Writing may be remembered after letter-to-sound linkages have become inaccessible, and it may facilitate retention of the skill. Tactile exercises might increase the likelihood of remembering letter sounds traced on a palm.

Teachers must prepare learners for this eventuality and stress the importance of practice, even if it is laborious and discouraging.

## Perceptual Learning, Discrimination of Varying Letter Patterns

Textbooks could present letters in sequences that would help detect critical features and distinguish minute details such as the number of dots on Arabic letters. To help focus on the correct dimensions, letters should initially be of the same type font. Also, letter or word patterns must be consistently linked to specific sounds or concepts. But in later lessons, various type fonts could be introduced, including handwriting. Discrimination training could progress from easy to hard, initially avoiding teaching together the letters that look similar, but eventually juxtaposing them, after learners have connected them frequently to sounds and seen them inside words.

Letters shaped differently from others (such as Latin X, Arabic k, or Hindi ksh) stand out and their sounds may be rapidly identified. Such salient letters can be introduced in textbooks and instruction and interspersed in such a way as to facilitate reading of other letters. People who still read serially can use such salient letters to search for words in texts or dictionaries that they otherwise do not recognize automatically.

Given the limited time of literacy instruction, writing often has a lower priority. It may be more effective to focus on building fluency in reading and then move to writing. Yet, writing may facilitate perceptual learning; significant motor and visuospatial abilities are reinforced through copying during basic reading instruction. Writing may also prevent forgetting. For this reason, tactile exercises may be given when letters are taught: learners may use their fingers to trace large models of letters, then they look at the letters and trace them with a pencil on their free palm while naming them. They may also trace letters by finger on a rough surface while repeating the sound.

Some reading problems are due to poor eyesight. Teachers could ask learners whether they can see certain designs on their books or on the blackboard and seat those who cannot see well nearer the blackboard.

## Utility of Literacy and Numeracy as Motivators

Group formation and a concrete or common goal facilitate staying in class and persevering. Also, livelihood training helps under rather limited circumstances to keep learners in class. To keep learners focused on a concrete goal, it should be shown early on how learners can use even rudimentary skills to improve their lives (such as looking for information in a newspaper, reading labels of drug bottles, and scrutinizing children's report cards). People are more likely to remember skills or material if they know what it will be used for.

Number recognition and calculations must also be automated. To achieve this, the units that are the building blocks of complex calculations, such as multiplication tables, could be memorized, but their use must be specifically demonstrated with local currency and transactions. Rather than focus on the abstract, which the unschooled may not handle well, calculations should focus on local currency and transactions. These should also help neoliterates avoid being cheated.

## Improving Use of Class Time

To attain the rate of 1–1.5 seconds per word, class time must be used much more efficiently. The frequently used method where one person reads and the others repeat does not offer sufficient practice in decoding skills. More effective use of time would be *reading in small groups* (reciprocal teaching). This means that teachers must learn grouping techniques and monitor learner groups for errors.

Teacher training is typically very short and must improve substantially, in terms of content as well as social issues. Training should include the basics of the cognitive principles needed to develop automaticity, phonological awareness, and working memory. However, the low education of teachers must be taken into account. One viable training means is to use videotaped role modeling, which would show examples of effective and ineffective instruction.

## Assessing Empowerment and Other Social Benefits

The social benefits of literacy have been hard to assess, and the one-time self-reports are unreliable measures of progress or sustainability. Program organizers must be quite clear about what empowerment benefits they should reasonably expect and how to bring them about. If a program has empowerment objectives, they should be worked into the curriculum timeframe, and teachers should be explicitly instructed on activities to be undertaken. To minimize memory bias of researchers and participants, baseline responses should be obtained to show change, including control groups if possible.

## Preparatory Skills to Facilitate Reading Acquisition

Perhaps all courses should devote much time in the first two weeks to preparatory tasks. These could be:

- Phonological awareness exercises for about 20 minutes daily.
- Learning to count through local money and transactions, discussing how to avoid being cheated.
- Digit span and other exercises (integrated within counting and phonological awareness) to help lengthen the working memory; understanding pictures in the textbook, using data in syllogisms.
- Simple visual tests to determine which learners might need to sit nearer the blackboard. (These could be included in one page of a textbook.)
- Creating a utility for literacy, for example, asking learners to bring in materials they would like to read.

It is important to find out which of the various paradigms discussed in this document are more effective in increasing reading speed and accuracy of adult neoliterates. Means may be found to apply those that are, at least in environments that can sustain them. Technology prices keep dropping, and solar energy makes computer operation possible in remote rural areas. Given the urgency to achieve Education for All by the year 2015, it may be deemed desirable to invest more in applied literacy research and in more efficient operation of literacy classes.

# 1
# Background: Adventures in Adult Literacy

Worldwide, nearly a billion adults, at least 600 million of them women, are illiterate.[1] Over 70 percent of them live in nine large countries: Bangladesh, Brazil, China, Egypt, India, Indonesia, Mexico, Nigeria, and Pakistan.[2] Most have been unschooled, but others are illiterate because of early dropout or inefficient schooling. The number of adult illiterates worldwide is larger than the number of primary-school students, who amount to roughly 700 million.

Adult literacy is highly relevant to poverty alleviation efforts worldwide, because in the twenty-first century much of the information needed to make decisions and improve one's economic, personal, family, or political conditions is presented in written form. People must be able to decipher a script code quickly, understand the contents of the documents, and decide upon options transmitted in them. For these reasons, reduction of adult illiteracy is an important component of the Education for All (EFA) initiative, a global effort to achieve universal completion of primary education by 2015 and eliminate gender disparities in education by 2005. Since the 1990 World Conference on Education for All, the World Bank has acknowledged and committed itself to expansion of quality education, including goals to: (a) reduce the 1990-level of adult illiteracy (23.8 percent male, 39.5 percent female) by half by the year 2015; and (b) expand the provision of basic education and training in other essential skills required by youth and adults.[3]

After a decade of effort, however, progress remains uneven and inadequate. Clearly, the EFA goals will not be met in at least 28 countries unless the pace sharply accelerates.[4] But the gap in information availability between the rich and the poor of the world may actually be widening.[5] Worldwide, over 100 million children are still out of school, and an undetermined number of others attend school for only 1 or 2 years. Instructional time in the schools of the poor tends to be limited, and dropouts are often illiterate. Unschooled or under-schooled children are the next generation of illiterate adults. So, as they slip through the schooling efforts, nonformal programs should be in place to capture them and efficiently teach them their country's literacy code and related basic skills.[6] Thus, *effective and efficient* instruction in basic adult literacy is needed more than ever.

Most developing countries acknowledge the need for continuing large programs in adult literacy and commit themselves to special efforts to eradicate literacy in the coming decade.[7] (For example, the government of Senegal would like to make one million adults literate per year.) However, the delivery of adult basic education has a long and disappointing history. In the 1960s–1970s, conventional wisdom regarded nonformal education as a cheap and rapid alternative to educate an entire population.[8] Many countries carried out literacy campaigns in that period, a time of considerable thinking into literacy theory and practice.[9] But these early programs offered government-led, top-down, and brief courses without follow-up and made few people literate. A minority of eligible participants enrolled, and of those about 50 percent dropped out. Of those who stayed on, about 50 percent passed literacy tests, and of those about 50 percent were estimated to have dropped back into illiteracy. Overall, many of the 1970s campaigns had efficiency rates of about 12.5 percent, with few participants acquiring stable literacy skills.[10] The ineffectiveness of those literacy programs dampened the interest of development agencies in this educational vehicle.

Until about 1990, World Bank nonformal education components were small. Bank lending for literacy was only about 1–3 percent of education lending. In most cases, the components accounted for less than 10 percent of the project costs, and even those amounts were often deleted from country budgets.[11] Perhaps because of Bank cost recovery policies at that time, there was almost no support for reading materials, library services, or audiovisual aids. There was also no strengthening of implementation capacity. A review of nonformal education projects approved in FY63–85 documented the limited support given to literacy components[12] and concluded that the results were due to neglect during appraisal and supervision. The authors recommended greater attention to the nonformal subsector, actual training of adults, more investment, and a focus on learner demand. However, the conclusions of the review were construed to mean that literacy and other subjects of nonformal education were ineffective investments, and almost no literacy projects were initiated for a decade.[13]

The difficulties of the early adult literacy programs prompted reflection in the donor community regarding the definition of literacy and whether adults really needed to be literate.[14] One school of thought argued that people need basic skills for living rather than literacy per se.

Also, an expectation developed that universal primary education would expand rapidly, and that literacy programs would be unnecessary, so many donors declined to finance them.[15] In the 1980s, however, it became obvious that access to primary education itself was linked to parental literacy and that universal primary education was going to take much longer than expected. Donors restarted literacy projects in the 1990s, trying to improve project designs. However, the Bank remained reluctant to finance literacy through the 1990s. Adult literacy was specifically not dealt with in the 1995 education sector strategy paper, though the authors acknowledged that adult illiteracy would remain a major problem.[16] This stance prompted some criticism that the institution was neglecting adult needs due to orthodox economic ideology, devotion to a narrow human capital theory, and need to appear a commercially viable institution.[17]

Between 1990 and 2002, the Bank financed only seven free-standing adult literacy projects. As of January 2002, adult literacy was a component in 14 other education, women in development, and rural development projects, of which six had closed. More Bank lending is in the pipeline. For example, Morocco is implementing a Learning and Innovation Loan in adult literacy, and the Poverty Reduction Strategy Papers (PRSPs) of countries such as Burkina Faso, Mauritania, and Uganda, mention adult literacy activities as a means of poverty alleviation. The Human Development Network education anchor (HDNED) has staff with an exclusive responsibility for nonformal education. Thus, there is a heightened interest in this subsector and the availability of a body of information from literacy programs worldwide. A review by the Bank's Operations Evaluation Department outlines Bank project activities during 1990s and evidence regarding their effectiveness.[18]

The review found outcomes hard to judge because data are sparse, hard to interpret, and vary considerably in quality. As with Bank projects, government and nongovernmental agencies have not kept records that enable reliable calculation of attendance, dropout, completion, and literacy attainment. Literacy acquisition is sometimes assessed through self-reports, but these have been shown to be unreliable. Self-confidence and empowerment are frequently cited benefits of literacy instruction, but these are typically assessed only once and through self-assessment, so long-term benefits cannot be ascertained. Of 32 literacy programs for which statistics were available, the median completion rate was 78 percent, median attendance (five programs only) was 62 percent, and pass rate of a final test was 56 percent. Relapse into illiteracy is rarely reported; some neoliterates can read years after instruction (for example the mainly previously schooled participants in Uganda), but only 12-60 percent of graduates sampled from other programs met literacy criteria later on (such as in Ajmer-India, Bangladesh, Kenya). Even when graduates remember the mechanics of reading, evidence suggests that they may understand little of what they read.

Unit costs reported in the sector documents also show large variance, depending on whether teachers are paid or whether ministry-level staff salaries are included. Volunteer teachers are hard to retain and replace, so the cheaper programs may be less efficient; however, the relationship between cost and acquisition of stable literacy skills has not been established. Overall, costs per participant tend to be seen as low, but costs per person made literate are considerably higher.

As in the 1980s, adult literacy programs make up 1–5 percent of government or donor budgets, and they remain severely underfunded in comparison to primary education and number of potential beneficiaries. Given the approximately one billion adult illiterates in the world, why are literacy projects not more extensively financed? The Bank- and other donor-financed projects can now more effectively reach large numbers of prospective participants. Course dropout and completion rates seem to have improved, but pass rates are about what they were 25 years ago, and long-term outcomes are uncertain. Literacy programs still have not made a significant difference in the literacy rates of client countries. The modest efficiency of the interventions may be one reason why governments and donors are still ambivalent about financing adult literacy. Programs are financed with the expectation that once taught, people will remain literate. However, retention of literacy skills seems unpredictable.[19] The limited outcomes have spurred lending for post-literacy, but few adults can take the time needed for continuing education, and there is some reluctance to continue to spending funds on the same beneficiaries.

The World Bank and other donors have few educational specialists and tend to focus on institutional and management issues. The strategy of the 1990s has been to let knowledgeable nongovernmental organizations (NGOs) do in literacy what they know best ("faire faire").[20] But the technical expertise of many NGOs is uncertain. A new paradigm is needed. Research on human memory now offers some clear avenues of action. Adults may learn to read better if offered the benefits of scientific research conducted in various parts of the world. However, government and NGO officials should become familiar with these concepts, and research is still needed to increase instructional effectiveness.

This document attempts to fulfill this purpose. It summarizes in understandable language state-of-the-art knowledge culled from the cognitive and neuropsychological research about how adult literacy can be taught most efficiently. It also presents information on instructional issues pertaining to efficient adult literacy instruction. It is hoped that this information will facilitate policy development and help decisionmakers make sensible resource allocation choices.

## Notes

1. Lind and Johnson 1990.
2. Aftab 1994, citing UNESCO reports.
3. Targets are country-specific. UNESCO 2000.
4. Education for Dynamic Economies, August 2001.
5. Comings, Smith, and Shrestha, undated.
6. UNESCO defines literacy as a person's ability "to read and write with understanding a short simple statement of his/her everyday life" (UNESCO Statistical Yearbook 2001). The terms "nonformal education" and "adult basic education" (ABE or "adult basic education and literacy"—ABEL) are often used interchangeably with "adult literacy." However, nonformal education includes all forms of deliberately organized education outside the mainstream education system. ABE may include bridges to the formal system or other skills.
7. Many country reports are shown on the UNESCO Web page, www.unesco.org.
8. Jones 1990.
9. For example, Couvert 1979, Hamadache and Martin 1986, King 1978, Scribner and Cole 1981, 1978.
10. UNESCO/UNDP 1976. The literacy programs discussed in this document were not random, and results may have been presented in an effort to neutralize the effects of socialist literacy campaigns (Jones 1988).
11. Romain and Armstrong 1987.
12. The review encompassed 92 nonformal education projects, of which 49 percent financed adult literacy, while 77 percent financed rural skills development and income generation. Only about 35 projects had significant nonformal education components. The eight adult literacy projects considered successful had strong country commitment, institutional support, strong materials support, and availability of counterpart funds (Romain and Armstrong, p. 35).
13. Lauglo 2001, p. 13.
14. Bennett 1995; Eisemon Marble, and Crawford 1995, 1999.
15. Iredale 1994.
16. World Bank 1995, p. ix; p 15.
17. Jones 1997, p. 370–372. (See also Jones 1988, 1990.)
18. Abadzi 2003a (forthcoming).
19. Educated, automatic readers seem to lack an intuitive understanding of the brain's functions and limitations and expect learners to perform better.
20. See, for example, Diagne 2001.

# 2
# Cognitive Science in the Service of Adult Literacy

Since the early 1990s, much research has focused on how people process reading information. Brain imaging technologies (such as fMRI and PET[1]) have made it possible to get glimpses of when and how various parts of the brain talk to each other. This type of reading research has been primarily motivated by the need to improve the performance of dyslexic children in developed countries. Most reading researchers work in Western Europe and the United States, where the spelling of English may exacerbate reading difficulties, and where funding is available to study them. Research studies have also been carried out on unschooled populations, such as the few older illiterates found in Portugal and Yugoslavia. These studies aimed to understand how literacy shapes the cognitive system, particularly the neural systems for spoken and written language.

The findings of this research should be pertinent to literacy instruction of unschooled adults, but thus far there has been little transfer of knowledge. Illiterates are in faraway Asia and Africa, and researchers usually do not speak their languages. Research funding has not been targeted to unschooled populations. Also, the terminology and complexity of the cognitive and neuropsychological publications limit this domain of knowledge to specialists. Thus, the challenge has been to find information useful in improving adult literacy programs and operationalize it.

To do so, the author contacted in 1999–2002 about 21 academics and researchers in fields that have reading applications. The researchers, interviewed in person or by phone, offered ideas, guidance, and references on how to speed up or make more efficient the instruction of unschooled adults in developing countries. The initial contacts led to new sources, hypotheses, inquiries, and research articles. The guidance and leads these academics provided is the basis for the material presented in this review.[2]

Presenting the concepts and findings for practitioners has been challenging. The cognitive and neuropsychological research often employs terminology incomprehensible to laymen (such as phonological awareness, geons, pseudowords) in complex sentences. Clear concepts are sometimes hard to present because statements about them are often qualified. These domains of research still have many questions to answer, data are scarce, and theories are still evolving. The missing puzzle pieces lead different scholars to different conclusions. Some publications raise more questions than they answer, while others probe concepts that are still not understood. This report minimizes the use of terminology and gives details or differing interpretations in the notes sections. The conclusions presented in this review have limitations, but this is how the cognitive implications for adult literacy instruction can be summarized in 2003.

Because illiterate adults face considerable problems in basic reading, this document focuses on the rudiments of literacy. It does not discuss extensively the acquisition of vocabulary and advanced reading comprehension.

## Human Evolution toward Efficient Reading

*Armed with quivers of poisoned arrows, a party of Southern African bushmen sets off on a hunt. The men walk fast, glancing down from time to time but barely breaking stride to observe the ground for tracks. The translator explains how they read the ground—"the same way you people read a book; the bush is our book." They can determine the age and sex of animals by reading the signs they leave behind. One young hunter drops to his heels and examines the droppings of a hartebeest; the more roughage the less efficient its digestion and the older the animal. A male springbok will often bring up the rear of the herd, and a male gemsbok will butt tree trunks with its horns to scent its territory.*

*Bushmen can measure the age of tracks by the time it takes termites to rebuild a nest that's been trampled on, or a blade of grass to spring back to its usual position, or a spider to repair its cobweb. When Bushmen hit an animal with an arrow, they don't immediately sprint after it; they go to where it was standing and memorize its particular footprint. Only then will they begin to patiently track it until it falls.*[3]

Bushmen recognize and process complex visual and auditory patterns whose existence is unimagined for those who have not been made "literate" in them. Furthermore, they decipher new variations of known patterns, as if they read someone else's scribbling. Scripts and books are only a few thousand years old, but the capacity for the functions involved in reading apparently has offered survival advantages throughout human evolution. Thus, the brain has parts that are pre-adapted for reading.[4] Studies from various countries suggest that some components of reading and learning to read are universal: extracting and using information about how frequently various letter and sound combinations occur, and automatization of basic processes. Others are more language-specific, such as the relationship between decoding a series of letters and comprehension of a message. There is still considerable debate on how close the relationship is between biology and reading skill.

One can think of the brain as a processing space, a malleable computer. At birth, much of the hardware is not hooked up and little of the software is running. Information is registered in multiple areas, and there is some redundancy, which is useful in case of brain damage. The same tissue participates in different mental functions. Location may differ from person to person, but generally, reading and spelling engage on a nerve network between the occipital, temporal, and inferior parietal cortex.[5]

The brain physically changes as it learns. Each change enables new learning and further changes, so there is constant evolution that is customized to experience.[6] If a skill is not used, it is lost. The brain also has optimal periods in early life for acquiring some skills. It was once thought that children's brains stopped developing early. But maturation continues at least into the teen years and the 20s. The brains of people in their later teens, ages 17 or so, are known to undergo considerable change that includes major expansion of many nerve networks as well as elimination of others.[7] It is conceivable that networks that have not been used by late adolescence (some of which may be related to effortless reading) are eliminated. However, the brain has more plasticity than was once believed, and neural connections continue to be made throughout life. Though there is a cost to learning later in life, the brain can still change in response to needs. Targeted training (such as forcing the paralyzed limbs of stroke victims to work) has been found to bring about learning and brain development in adults that was once unexpected.

## A Fundamental Problem: Cognitive Limitations of Unschooled People

Learning a specific skill, such as reading and writing during childhood, creates profound changes in brain architecture. So, the difference between literates and illiterates does not just consist of a reading skill. Schooled people have neural networks that the unschooled lack. These *are related to memory, attention span, data use, and ultimately decisionmaking.*

Some research on how unschooled people think started in 1931–32, when the Russian psychologist Alexander Luria interviewed illiterates in the former Soviet Union. He found that illiterates tended to rely on their or their elders' experience and might be less likely to use data received on the spot for deductive reasoning. For example, an illiterate Uzbek villager from Kashgar was asked the following: "In the far north, where there is snow, all bears are white. Novaya Zemlya is in the far north. What color are the bears there?" The villager refused to answer because he had never been to Novaya Zemlya.[8] More recent research indicated that illiterates rely more on concrete facts or consensus than people do with four years of education. For example, an illiterate person presented with the syllogism "All women in Mexico City are beautiful. My friend is from Mexico City. Is she beautiful?" may reply, "Of course she is because you like beautiful women." The unschooled much more easily solve arithmetic problems involving real-world situations (such as merchandise) than abstract questions, such as 15 + 19. They are also likely to categorize concepts differently from schooled people, and are less likely to use higher-order and lower-order categories.[9] If asked what a duck is, for example, a schooled individual would say that it is an animal or a bird; an illiterate might say that it is edible or that he killed one the day before.

Normal unschooled people have no deficiencies, they perform as they have throughout history. But schooled people have acquired cognitive "efficiencies" that give them certain advantages. Reading affects the interaction between the visual and language systems,[10] so language use is modified through literacy. Teachers pose hypothetical questions and ask students to use available data, so syllogisms and categorization skills are learned in schools. Schooled people use these skills in daily life (for example, to compare loan interest rates), while illiterates lack such mental tools.

Research studies, often using older Portuguese women as subjects, have illustrated some ways in which the brains of adult illiterates are wired differently:

- Illiterates show less dominance of the left hemisphere of the brain in language than literate people[11] and are likely to be more affected by strokes on speech centers. The brain activity of illiterates monitored by PET scans while doing language tasks tended to be more localized, and its locations were different.[12] (See brain scan example in Figure 1.) For example, when listening to real words, literates and illiterates performed similarly.[13] But illiterates had more difficulty repeating artificial words (pseudowords) correctly. PET scans showed that they did not activate the same neural structures as literates. Though illiterates have normal language development, they do not usually understand how phonemes make up words (phonological awareness—see below).
- The cognitive effects of schooling extend to complex sentences and decontextualized, *abstract speech*. There is evidence that many illiterates (like some dyslexics) cannot completely understand what radio

# Figure 1. Example of Functional Brain Organization Differences between Literates and Illiterates

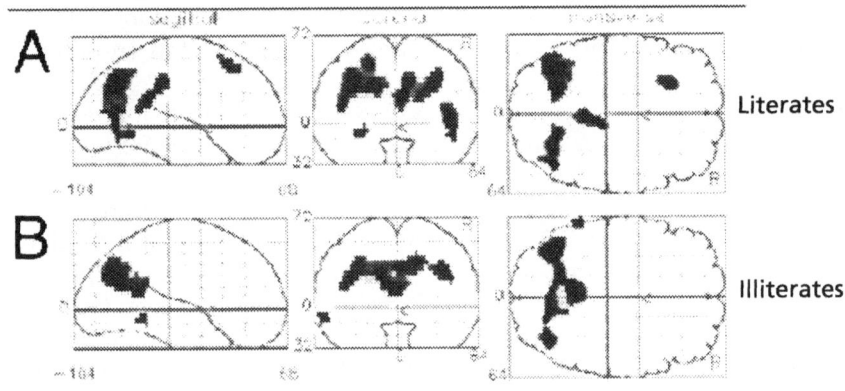

*Note:* Measurements of regional cerebral blood flow through a PET scanner while literate and illiterate subjects repeated actual words or pseudowords. Sagittal (side view), coronal (view from top), and transverse views are shown.
*Source:* Adapted from Castro-Caldas et al. 1998.

broadcasts say, even if they are in the same language or dialect and have a familiar context. Comprehension can improve some after six months of literacy instruction and even more after nine months.[14] However, if illiterates do not understand well the meaning of complex or abstract speech, they may not understand certain messages directed at the poor, such as AIDS prevention, and thus may miss out on some development interventions.

- The level of literacy also influences the ability to identify three-dimensional figures (called *visuospatial discrimination*), such as recognizing and naming pictures of objects (which exist in school books) in newspapers, or posters.[15] Women may be at a particular disadvantage. Research carried out on Mexican illiterates showed that women scored less well than men in tests such as drawing a cube.
- *The unschooled perform less well in numerical abilities*[16] *and in most memory tasks:* recalling a series of digits backward and forward, remembering 10 words, reproducing a short story, reproducing complex figures that were presented, recalling common objects, remembering sequences. Only in repeating simple sentences do they perform as well as literate people. Possibly, they do less well because the memory functions of literates are stretched in school.[17]
- Changes in cognition during life are affected by education. *The first three grades of (relatively effective) schooling seem to have the most significant*

*effect* on these cognitive variables; subsequent grades have a decreasing effect. The attention span decreases as people age, but education influences cognition more than aging; differences among age groups are smaller than differences among education groups. People with limited education perform neuropsychological tests best at an older age than highly educated subjects.[18]

- The memory and visuospatial skills, which illiterates perform less well, influence general thinking. They are important *in decisionmaking and judgment*: mental accounting, perceptions of risk, the consideration of context on making judgments, comparisons, use of reference points, cognitive biases, and the communication and sharing of information relevant to decisionmaking. A very short working memory limits the use of practical strategies to perform many mental tasks. (See more below.) The tendency to rely on consensus and environmental validation limits the likelihood of using new data in decisionmaking, so the unschooled may obtain most information from authority figures.

Less efficient decisionmaking probably has *consequences for poverty alleviation*. For example, villagers may attend a meeting and hear community development options available from an emergency social fund or receive agricultural extension messages. But they may fail to follow the verbal presentation or identify the diagrams presented; they may forget some of the alternatives offered, focus on those favored by their elders, and reject others or fail to follow up on some attractive alternatives. Thus, they may be unable to take full advantage of the opportunities offered.

Unless the cognitive limitations of illiterates are taken into account, development agencies may overestimate the effectiveness of poverty interventions. To target benefits and communicate them better, it may be worthwhile to tailor messages to the decisionmaking process of the unschooled. For example, reliance on consensus strengthens the rationale for group formation, which has been used extensively for microcredit and literacy. Decision theory and related cognitive research can help model likely decisions of the unschooled in various issues given sources of data, so that messages and resources can be provided more efficiently. Thus, better projects can be designed for the illiterate poor.

Clearly, reading and neuropsychological functions are correlated, but the exact cause-and-effect relationship between them is still unclear. Therefore, efforts were made to find out if cognitive functions could improve through direct training as part of a literacy program. A *neuropsychologically oriented literacy program* (called Neuroalfa) was developed to raise the performance of illiterates in Colima, Mexico.[19] The program involved 21 learners, ages 16–50 (mean age 33). It consisted of 34 exercises grouped in 10 lessons, each lesson requiring 3–4 hours, and each exercise requiring about one hour. The total instructional time was 40 hours, offered in three months, three times weekly. Besides basic literacy, it taught phonological awareness, semantic categorization, finding similarities, interpreting objects drawn on paper, verbal memory, and abstracting abilities. Learners practiced reciting digits backwards and forwards, serial recall of unrelated strings of words, story recall, and the repetition of artificial words. Another exercise was to read a story and direct listeners to remember the last word of each sentence. Contrary to many literacy programs, writing was used extensively to reinforce visualization in three-dimensional space. Results were compared to those of two traditional methods of teaching literacy. After literacy training, the experimental group improved in most neuropsychological tests (though not in motor function tests), and it had higher reading scores, particularly in comprehension. It also improved in time orientation, calculation, and deducing the sequences of various figures, which had not been specifically practiced. However, the sustainability of the new skills has not been explored.

### *Implications for Training*
### Expanding Cognitive Skills

Neuropsychological exercises can potentially improve memory, attention, verbal skills, or hypothesis formation. It is unclear in which areas they are more effective, whether improvement is sustainable, how to bring it about faster, and what resources are needed. However, research points to two paradigms:

The Neuroalfa literacy method could be refined and tried more extensively. Its exercises are not complex and could be presented in a separate booklet for teachers if studies point to their long-term utility in improving the memory and syllogistic capacity of neoliterates as well as reading scores. This program would add to the length of a literacy class. Research is also needed to determine how sustainable these skills are and how well they transfer to daily thinking and decisionmaking.

Techniques of participatory rural appraisal and empowerment could be modified to improve some cognitive limitations of illiterates. The Participatory Rural Appraisal (PRA) technique and related REFLECT methodology, used by NGOs like ActionAid, employ similar techniques. PRA facilitators use visual materials to help the poor articulate their existing knowledge. Materials are produced by the participants (such as maps, calendars, matrices, diagrams), who choose a local issue to discuss and improve it by "working collectively" and "producing actively." The REFLECT method extends PRA to reading. Though the method appears to be of limited use in teaching basic reading,[20] it may improve spatial orientation and verbal fluency.

## Skills Important for Efficient Reading

- You are at a bus stop hoping to catch a bus to your village. As you sit there, a bus comes fast around the corner. Is it the right bus? You must read its destination label within 1–2 seconds and if it is, flag it down.
- You are a rural Nepali borrowing money from a moneylender, who has scribbled a document and asks you to sign it. He reads it aloud, but is he truthful? At a time of considerable anxiety, you must be able to read the moneylender's handwriting fast and correctly or lose your livelihood.
- You are looking at one of the informational pamphlets that have been developed after much social research on how to save people like you from AIDS. You have been to literacy class, and you sound out the words of the first page. By the time you reach the end of a sentence, do you remember how it started and what its message was?
- You are an educated Norwegian who went to work in Thailand, became fluent in Thai, and learned to read its syllabic script. As you watch television, you see letters passing at the bottom of the screen that warn of an impending hurricane. Are you able to decipher them at the speed they travel, understand the message, and take cover?

These instances require one to read fast and effortlessly, a function that seems deceptively easy. For years, reading acquisition has been a black box, prompting various theories as to how people should best learn to read. The research is opening the black box. Therein lies in a tangle of visual and auditory networks, which create interrelated functions that are still being explored. The letter shapes are related to previous visual and auditory memories with many checks and feedback points. Every moment of reading involves interpreting print through neural networks that assign sound to the letters and bring meaning from the lexicon, the language dictionary that develops in the brain throughout life. When a word does not make sense, the reader sounds it out in an effort to connect it to the lexicon and may bring in alternative interpretations to make sense of the message. An expert reader does this within milliseconds, without being conscious of the process. How does this happen?

### The Decoding Process

Four cognitive mechanisms help figure out the message:[21] the phonological, orthographic, semantic, and context processors. As a string of letters is read, the phonological processor determines whether it is pronounceable. If it is, the phonological processor will signal the orthographic processor of that fact and prod the semantic processor for possible interpretations. Then the context processor will give connotations and alternative meanings, given the topic of the text. If a string of letters is not pronounceable, the phonological processor will stimulate the orthographic processor to bring up alternative visual patterns until a reasonable identification is made. If a letter is read wrong, the semantic processor signals to the phonological processor that the word does not make sense, and the phonological processor tries again. The cycle may be repeated until a passage is understood or the reader gives up (Figure 2).

## Figure 2. Major Processes Involved in Reading Comprehension

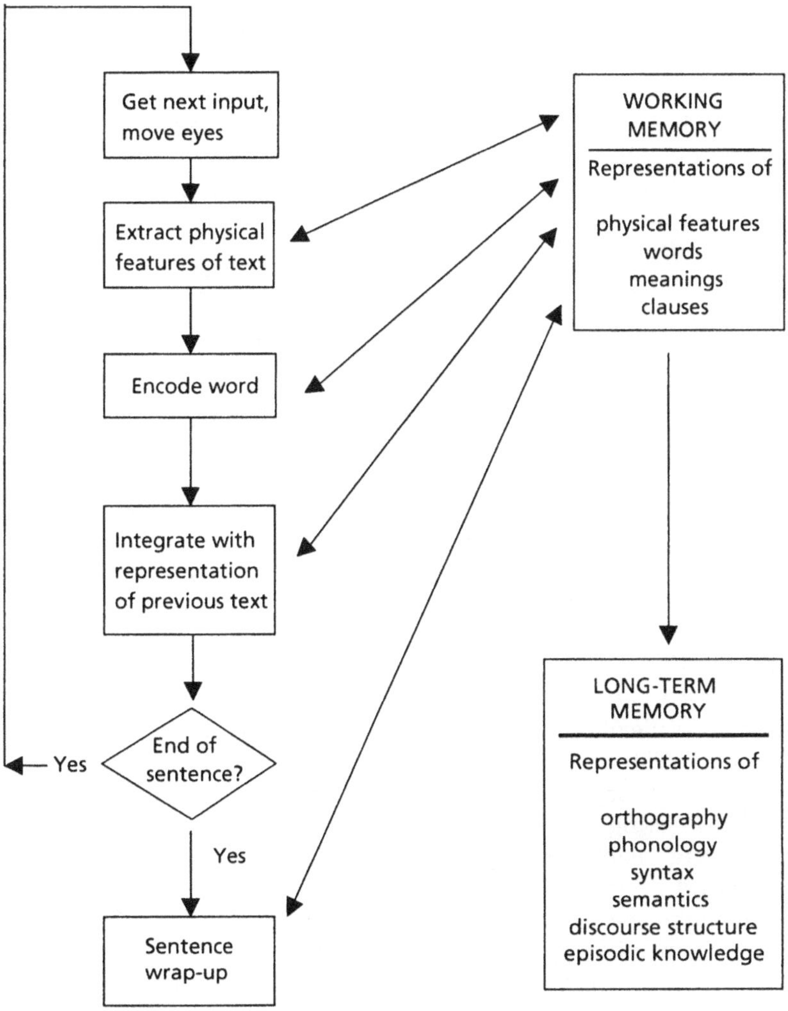

```
┌─────────────────┐              ┌─────────────────────┐
│ Get next input, │─────────────▶│   WORKING MEMORY    │
│   move eyes     │              ├─────────────────────┤
└────────┬────────┘              │  Representations of │
         ▼                       │                     │
┌─────────────────┐              │  physical features  │
│ Extract physical│◀────────────▶│       words         │
│ features of text│              │      meanings       │
└────────┬────────┘              │      clauses        │
         ▼                       └──────────┬──────────┘
┌─────────────────┐                         │
│  Encode word    │◀───────────▶            │
└────────┬────────┘                         │
         ▼                                  ▼
┌─────────────────┐              ┌─────────────────────┐
│ Integrate with  │◀────────────▶│   LONG-TERM MEMORY  │
│ representation  │              ├─────────────────────┤
│ of previous text│              │  Representations of │
└────────┬────────┘              │                     │
         ▼                       │     orthography     │
       ◇ End of ◇ ──Yes──┐       │      phonology      │
       ◇sentence?◇       │       │        syntax       │
         │Yes            │       │      semantics      │
         ▼               │       │  discourse structure│
┌─────────────────┐      │       │  episodic knowledge │
│    Sentence     │◀─────┘       └─────────────────────┘
│    wrap-up      │
└─────────────────┘
```

*Source:* Sekuler and Blake 2001, p. 255, adapted from Just and Carpenter 1980.

What is required for the four processors to operate effectively? A perception of letters relatively free of errors, reliable connection of various letters to sounds, and knowledge of the rules that put the two together.[22]

Letter combinations do not get recognized in a vacuum. The brain seems set up to learn which stimuli are useful for identifying meaningful reading symbols in a language.[23] When people become expert readers, they rely on familiarity and meaning to extract information. They are more accurate in perceiving a word as a whole than in perceiving its isolated components. If they see disconnected words, they take twice as long to read them.[24] They are also not bothered by artistic letters, unless these become too distorted, and then their reading rate slows down.

Beginning readers quickly learn the frequency of various letters and which letter combinations are most likely.[25] Thus, beginners use their phonological processor early on to sound out words. However, they cannot process the letters fast or accurately enough and rely on meaning and context excessively, as they try to guess from one or two letters what they are reading. The process of reading takes up all their attention, and little is left for the message.

As beginners get more practice, they develop a store of symbols, words, and word patterns that can be accessed rapidly for recognition of words encountered in each reading task. A reader is increasingly able to discriminate the relevant features of stimuli, and the units that are recognized become larger and larger. The focus on individual meaningful words means that letters are recognized faster in real words than in nonsense strings of letters. This phenomenon, called the *word superiority effect*,[26] has important implications for beginning readers. If they can identify a word they are trying to read, they are better able to identify the letters in it, even though they may not know some of them well. The recognition in turn reinforces practice and knowledge about these letters.[27] Because the internal dictionary facilitates decoding, people must become literate in a language they know well.

Though the language knowledge greatly facilitates decoding of the passages, recognition of the letter patterns is very important (more on this later). A little of both skills is needed in the beginning, and one builds on the other. With partial recognition of some letters, a learner may access the internal dictionary and "guesstimate" the likely pronunciation of a word. But to bring up the correct words and make sense of a message, fast and accurate letter recognition is necessary. Even mild difficulties in word identification can pull attention away from the underlying meaning, reduce the speed of reading, and create the need to reread selections to grasp the meaning.[28] *If the reading speed drops below 100 words per minute (about 1.8 words per second), the demands on the memory increase and interfere with comprehension.*[29]

The prosody of words, such as stress on syllables and voice tones is also important in decoding. At times, poor readers can accurately decode a word but cannot recognize it because they have not correctly accented one of the syllables.[30] Thus, it may be harder for beginning readers to decode tonal languages when the tone is not indicated in the script, such as in many African languages.

Because words form the basic unit of reading recognition, it has been tempting to teach children to recognize whole words as entire units. Many children learn this way, particularly those that get parental help. Phonetic decoding (phonics) is overall a more effective method, particularly for students at risk for reading failures and those with reading difficulties.[31] The "whole word" seems not to benefit adults, possibly due to certain difficulties with perceptual learning (see below). It has been employed by the REFLECT program of the ActionAid NGO.[32] Indian participants learned to recognize pictorially a few common words that they saw in street signs (such as "stop"), but could not break them down or recognize those letters in different configurations.

### Implications for Instruction
### Decoding and Skilled Reading

Much of the literacy class should be devoted to guidance and practice in decoding. To bring about skilled reading, instruction must help learners efficiently and quickly understand words and offer an analytical strategy for learning new words.

Decoding techniques are often language- or script-specific, but many exercises have been devised, such as (a) phonographix, a system to show extensions of reading rules to similar patterns[33] (mat – cat – hat – ham – him), (b) reading pseudo-words that look like real words, and (c) speed-reading letters together, though they constitute nonsense syllables.

To get the benefit of the word superiority effect, textbooks and teachers might reduce the presentation of unconnected letters and include early on the letters in words. New letters could be presented before and after words that include them (for example, paper, e, p, a, r). New texts could consist of words that have already been presented or have well-practiced letter patterns.

Often, literacy classes present mnemonics to help learners connect letters and sounds (such as the Laubach method, which creates mnemonics such as "a is for apple"). The benefits and costs of mnemonics are unclear. They may cause learners to make irrelevant connections rather than the instant and effortless connections that are needed between letters and sounds. On the other hand, reminders of how letters look may help learners in the very beginning or later if they lapse into illiteracy (more on this later). Mnemonics may create more stable connections if learners themselves make them up according to their existing knowledge.

People (adults and children) must become literate in a language they know well. If they do not know the meaning of many words used in class, they will see fewer identifiable words, and they will be deprived of the letter-level reinforcement that they would receive from known words. The difficulty posed by foreign languages is greater if these have complex spelling, as is the case with English and French.

## Working Memory: The Reading Comprehension Bottleneck

The pieces of information extracted by the processors from the text are stored in the short-term memory, also known as working memory. While there, they enable the reader to make decisions about or recognize words while remembering what has just been read and retrieving more information if needed. Getting the text information quickly is very important, because the brain has some strict processing time limits. *The working memory is quite short*; in educated people it lasts about 12 seconds and holds about 7 items. If the information is not consciously rehearsed in this period, it is erased and replaced with new items (Figure 3).

Unskilled readers cannot put messages into their long-term memory fast enough and are trapped by the short duration of the working memory. Within about 12 seconds, a reader must read a sentence (or a complete grammatical unit), process its meaning, classify it in cognitive networks where knowledge exists about the same topic, and go on. If a sentence has about six words, this means that people must *be able to read at least one word per second (or per 1.5 second at the outset) in order to be functional readers*.[34] If they read more slowly, they find that they have forgotten the beginning of a sentence by the time they reach the end. All the attention is taken up with decoding, and none is left for the message (Figure 3). If readers must consciously search their memory for letters values, then their working memory is cluttered by individual letters. When they make mistakes and misread a word, they must start all over.

Literacy course graduates may read too slowly. For example, graduates sampled in Burkina Faso were found to read one word per 2.2 seconds and were correct only 80–87 percent of the time (Annex A). At this speed

## Figure 3. Time Required for Reading

### Consequences of Slow Reading

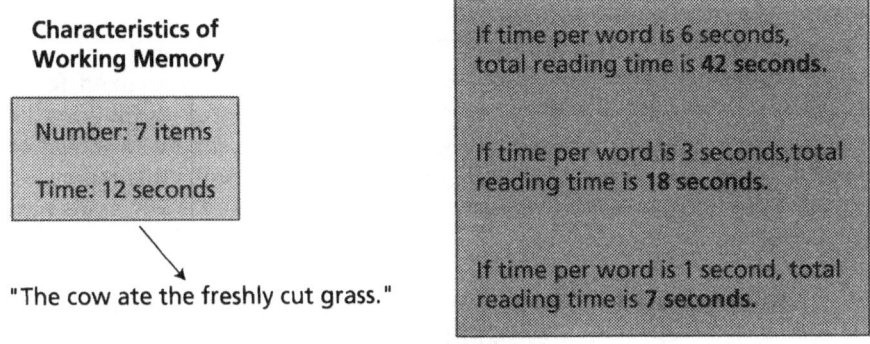

*Source:* Lecture materials (James M. Royer, Ph.D, 2000).

and error rate the short-term memory is overwhelmed. To function even marginally, a reader should have 91–95 percent accuracy.[35] Many neoliterates may be discouraged by this punishing act and avoid reading, thus risking a lapse back into illiteracy. However, a person who manages to read a sentence within the duration of working memory may be encouraged to go on. *This speed of 1–1.5 seconds per word is a critical limit that may determine who will remain a functional reader after the end of a literacy course and who will not.* This rate corresponds merely to oral-reading norms for grade 1 children.[36] But even this speed rate has a caveat: The unschooled are known to have shorter working memory, so they may have less time to process a sentence than educated people.[37]

Given the realities of working memory, reading tests at the end of various literacy programs may overestimate readers' skills. During these tests, learners are given a limited amount of text to process in plenty of time. The examinee may read a passage repeatedly until it is pieced together. But in real life, readers may not have the inclination or time to save material again and again in working memory and may abandon reading. Neoliterates may pass tests and still be unable to function as literates. Therefore, literacy program statistics may not represent actual ability to decode material in daily life.

This cognitive limitation has not been taken into account in the various definitions of literacy, notably UNESCO's definition that someone literate can "to read a write with understanding a short simple statement of his/her everyday life."[38] Furthermore, literacy in the twenty-first century encompasses much more complex tasks than decades ago, when the term "functional literacy" was coined.[39] There is a widespread need to decode large amounts of text that may be moving or written in stylized fonts (such as on computer screens in airports), which challenge the skills of literacy class graduates. Clearly, higher levels of performance are needed now. If functional literacy is defined as having sufficient skills to process information, the number of people worldwide who lack basic skills may be as high as 2 billion.[40]

### Implications for Instruction and Policy on Adult Literacy
### Working Memory

Long-term memory is like a huge bottle that has an opening the width of a pin. Short-term memory holds very little information at a time, and it constantly gets wiped out. To insert the required chunks of information into the bottle, the information must go through very fast. Letter-by-letter reading uses up working memory, while faster reading uses less. If the reading speed drops below 100 words per minute (about 1.8 word per second) the demands on memory increase and interfere with comprehension. This is why fast and effortless recognition is critical for reading comprehension.

The necessity to read within the limits of working memory determines who is a functional literate in real life and points towards a *minimum standard for literacy acquisition*: Course participants should learn to read at a rate of a word per 1–1.5 second with about 95 percent accuracy. Those who read below this threshold may later forget how to read.

Because reading time is of essence, literacy tests must be timed. Slow readers who may take the time to decipher a passage during a testing session may not have the time, patience, or attention span to read the same passage in daily life.

It is not sufficient for literacy courses merely to teach decoding; graduates must acquire a rapid reading rate, or their skills may not be very useful. To achieve these rates, it may be necessary for literacy programs to teach more extensive courses with better trained teachers and higher budgetary outlays than is currently the case.

## Automaticity: Means to Overcome the Working Memory Bottleneck

The brain has the means to overcome the narrow limits of working memory. To make sense of anything but the most rudimentary text, a person must become an automatic reader. Reading automaticity is the ability to perceive entire words and recognize them within milliseconds. Words become units, are seen as "encapsulated," and are read very fast regardless of length. Like bike riding or smoking, reading is one of many perceptual and motor functions that become automated when a person repeats them. This ability allows the brain to focus on a whole function rather than its nuts and bolts. Thus, there seems to be a paradox: letter-by-letter reading uses up working memory, while faster reading uses less.

The practice of almost any cognitive or motor skill creates profound changes in the brain and changes the location where skills are stored. Automatized functions tend to be stored not in the cerebral cortex, where conscious movement, thinking, and judgments take place, but in deeper brain circuits, such as the basal ganglia. How a function is transferred from conscious (cortical) to the unconscious (subcortical) control is not well understood. But because of the change in brain location, novice and skilled performers use two qualitatively different forms of information processing.

The performance of novices requires effort and conscious decisions. But when a skill becomes automatic, it is difficult to hold back its performance. The right stimulus brings out the automatic behavior, so an educated person reads without trying. Once automatized, a behavior cannot be easily forgotten.[41] *Automatic readers do not normally lapse back into illiteracy.*

The effortlessness of expert reading has been used to test automaticity since the 1930s.[42] For example, students would be asked the color of the print of words in lists of colored words. They were asked to ignore what was printed. However, the word 'red' printed in green ink, for example, often resulted in marked delays before students said "green."[43] In the 1980s, automaticity was described in statistical regression terms. Its existence was determined on the basis of the slope of the function relating decision time to the number of items either in memory, or in a visual display. Experimental subjects practiced learning various types of stimuli, such as recognizing many visual displays. When multiple items could be processed in the same amount of time as one single item, then the function was considered automated.[44] In the twenty-first century, researchers look for automaticity through brain imaging techniques in conditions that promote visual perceptions of reading with limited involvement of the prefrontal lobe of the cortex, which is engaged when constructing novel thought or response sequences required for complex thinking. Brain imaging studies and single cell recordings in monkeys show that mastery of a skill, such as reading, results in less cortical activation than processing of novel stimuli.[45]

## Serial and Parallel Processing

Initially people read serially, one letter at a time. As they move into automatic reading, they process more letters or entire words "in parallel."[46,47] Reading larger chunks at a time enables people to use appropriate phrasing and intonation when reading aloud. Readers who recognize the text and get its meaning in fractions of a second are likely to stay in the parallel mode. But there is difficulty in discriminating letters or understanding words, readers resort to serial processing (for example, to read a foreign word, such as the name "Tchaikovsky"). Good readers use both serial and parallel processing and unconsciously choose the right type to use according to the readability of letters, word difficulty, word length, context, spelling, or consistency of the material. Expert readers access multiple sources of information in parallel and evaluate them while trying to recognize words. Some sources, such as visual feature information, are available before other sources, such as semantic content. When a sufficient threshold of certainty is reached, a decision is made about what a text says.[48]

*Building up recognition speed* is particularly important for beginning readers. The challenge in literacy classes is how to make recognition of many words automatic, so that sentences can be decoded within the limits of working memory. No research exists to show how many learners reach this stage, but they may be a small fraction. Persons living in low-literacy environments who learned to read in primary school, may have limited opportunities to practice, and they may have automatized reading functions only partially. Informal observations of rural residents who learned reading in the frequently inefficient rural primary schools (for example, middle-aged Bangladeshi rural women who mainly read for religious purposes) suggest that they may read slowly but fluently, with little effort and with the appropriate intonation. This may indicate that they understand the text and do not make a conscious effort to remember letter values. These people may read aloud or subvocally, possibly to refresh the items stored in working memory and prevent the message from being lost. They may be processing a word per 1–2 seconds and thus fitting sentences into their working memories. This may be possibly the historical level of skill among literate people.[49] Perhaps elimination of sounding out and connection directly to the brain's dictionary of meanings takes place with much more practice, which has become common only in recent years.

*Overlearning of small units may help automaticity.* Skilled reading is dependent on the development of fast and accurate reading of small units: letters, syllables, and common words. Extensively practicing and overlearning small units was shown to be effective in increasing speed and accuracy for children with reading difficulties.[50] Thus, weak readers are often drilled on small units and common words in hopes of learning to recognize them automatically. The same strategies may help neoliterates to read automatically the words they are likely to see often, even if they do not read the less frequent words or word endings automatically. The hope is that automaticity will eventually be extended to larger units and words, and that ultimately sentences can be read within the working memory span.

### Implications for Instruction
### Automaticity

A means to achieve reading automaticity is to give practice, starting with smaller words and proceeding to longer ones. A learner may read as fast as possible a list or a pack of cards showing 20 common words. (Sheets may also be used, but learners may learn the order of the words.) This may be done once per session, and the time may be recorded every day. When learners show no further improvement, they get a new list of longer words. Along with the new words, interspersed practice is given on the ones mastered earlier, to maintain old skills and build new ones. This method has been tried effectively in Burkina Faso. Learners who had been exposed to it performed better in reading tests than learners in a control group (Annex A). It remains unclear, however, how quickly automatic reading of individual words results in parallel processing of entire sentences and paragraphs.

Other techniques exist to force increasingly faster reading. For example, chanting—a quick turn taking reading rhythmically with a teacher or peer—may force students to deal with larger amounts of print faster than they otherwise would.

Computers may help learners read faster.[51] To achieve automaticity, extensive practice of varying materials is needed as well as consistent mapping of letter patterns to sounds. Adults may require multiple trials of pairing sounds with letter combinations (perhaps hundreds or thousands), and the usual literacy classes have neither the time nor the materials for such work. If computers are available, however, this work is feasible. Computerized presentations may engage learners and motivate them to stay and work at the tasks longer than they would otherwise do in a class.[52] This tool may also be very useful in post-literacy classes.

Thus far, literacy has been carried out exclusively with print, and the poorest countries cannot support large-scale computerized instruction in the medium term. However, India, Brazil, and South Africa can support high-technology media, have large numbers of computers in schools, and still have many illiterates. Literacy classes could make some use of available computer rooms. If computerized literacy instruction is shown to improve outcomes substantially, governments and donors might plan for larger-scale use in countries that gradually acquire school computers. Some computerized applications may work on cheaper equipment.[53]

## Phonological Awareness—Ability to Break Down Words

Beginning readers must learn to match the series of characters they see with word representations they have in their memory. To do that, they must understand where various words start and end. The ability to read new words comes only from knowledge of how orthography relates to sound.[54]

Phonological (or phonemic) awareness is the understanding that spoken language is made up of discrete sounds.[55] It seems to facilitate rapid visual recognition; thus it is the best predictor of how easily children will learn to read, better than IQ, vocabulary, and listening comprehension.[56] Phonological awareness also results from learning to read, so the concept may just reflect basic information processing limitations. Children learning to read in phonetically spelled languages (such as Turkish) are more proficient in phonological tasks than English-speaking children.[57] Without phonological awareness, deciphering the code becomes a struggle. People who have this difficulty, called the *core phonological deficit*, find it harder to learn decoding and do not see properly and the letter patterns that allow the acquisition of rapid, automatic visual recognition. Many U.S. adults with low literacy skills cannot quickly segment spoken words into separate sounds. If readers cannot relate spelling to sound well, they are forced to play a guessing game that is misleading and discouraging.[58]

Phonological awareness tasks require retention of an acoustic string in memory, segmentation of that string at a phoneme level, and (usually) retrieval of a substring, either as a new word or as a sound. Training consists of deleting the initial or final vowels or consonants, counting the number of syllables (as appropriate in various languages), or rhyming. The skill can be taught to children and adults in a few days or weeks, and adults rapidly improve in it.[59] These tasks place large demands on short-term or working memory and attention, thus offering practice in these important processes. One question that remains is whether training is sustainable or whether learners lose it if they do not use it. But learners clearly need training in learning to decode, and teaching them the skill directly has a value.

Several experiments have been made with adult illiterates and phonological awareness. Teaching how to segment words into phonemes improved the reading scores of Moroccan Arabs in French literacy classes[60] as well as older Portuguese illiterate farmers.[61] Also, neoliterates were much better in this skill than illiterates.[62] Adults acquire this skill more easily than children do.[63] The skill may help children and adults to predict the frequency of various letter combinations in their languages, as well as unusual combinations. Phonological awareness is less needed and is not well developed among people who only read Chinese.[64]

Phonological awareness training was put to a test in literacy classes of Burkina Faso; it was found that learners who had been exposed to it performed better in reading tests than learners in a control group, although their course had lasted less time than expected. Deleting initial and final vowels and consonants or breaking up words in syllables and counting the syllables were shown to be techniques that are also possible for teachers with limited education to master (Annex A).

### *Implications for Instruction*
### *Phonological Awareness*

Phonological awareness has been shown repeatedly to be effective in increasing the reading scores of neoliterates. The tasks of deleting the initial or final vowels or consonants, counting the number of syllables or rhyming can be easily taught to teachers and students. However, this type of training is not yet a staple of literacy programs. Phonological exercises are particular to various languages, and language specialists must determine how words must be segmented. Institutionalizing this method means writing brief manuals on the exercises, explaining their utility, and training teachers in their application.

The renowned Brazilian educator, Paulo Freire, used "generative" words derived from people's daily problems to create awareness of syllables, constructing and then deconstructing new words from them. His method has had social appeal for decades. Rather than use random words, phonological awareness exercises could include likely "generative" words. They could be more interesting and memorable for learners.

## Perceptual Learning and the Nitty-Gritty of Recognizing Letters

### Eye Movements and Expert Reading

When expert readers see a word, they usually process it as unit, not each letter separately. Eye movements and fixations help extract information from a page. The eyes jump (or *saccade*) as gaze shifts from one object to another, but they are relatively still between saccades. The number of saccades and fixations depends on the skill of the reader and difficulty of the text. The average fixation lasts about 250 milliseconds (msec), but may be 100–500 msec. The distance traveled by one saccade (which lasts 100 msec) is often about 3–4 letters to the left and 14–15 letters to the right for readers of English (Figure 4). Though about 90 percent of the time the eyes travel in one direction, there may be backward glances to check ambiguous text. An average reader reading average text reads about 1.1 words

**Figure 4. Eye Movements and Reading Time**

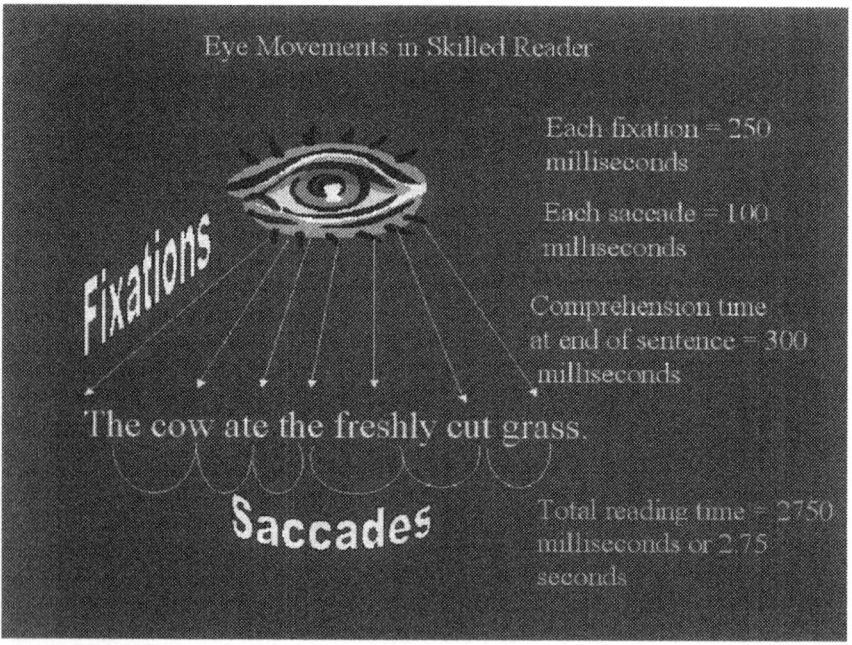

*Source:* Lecture materials (James M. Royer, Ph.D, 2000).

per fixation. While the eyes are fixed on print, the person interpreting text makes predictions about the words that may come next in a sentence, and plans the next saccade. Expert readers read at least 3.3 words per second or about 200 words per minute. By comparison, the beginners' eye movements are quite different. Their saccades are much shorter, around three letter spaces, they may make 2–3 fixations per word, and average fixation durations are much longer, 300–400 msec; they glance back much more often, so up to 50 percent of their eye movements are regressions.[65]

Fixation speed depends on people's decoding speed, so slow fixations are a symptom rather than a cause. However, research on aging adults (ages 62–75), who were skilled readers, showed that they could be trained to read more efficiently. Results included a reduced number of fixations and regressions per 100 words, increased average span of recognition and improved reading rate without loss of comprehension.[66] The challenge is to bring about similar improvements in beginning readers.

## *Recognizing Letter Patterns*

To understand a message fast, the visual patterns that make it up must first be recognized even faster. How are they recognized? Exact mechanisms are unknown. As mentioned earlier, perhaps the mind recognizes images by analyzing them and matching them to prototypes stored in memory and connecting them to sound. As a reader becomes proficient, sound at some point is bypassed, and there is more direct connection between the print and the internal dictionary of meanings in the brain; expert readers do not sound out words to recognize them, but if the text is difficult or ambiguous, people sound it out under their breath.[67] Most modern theories of memory assume direct access to meanings, though not necessarily in a single step.[68] For example, a literacy learner must first recognize that characters presented share features with stored prototypes, while at the same time attempting to recall all possible correlates of this prototype. The process takes time, because there are multiple cues, which can be associated with the prototypes. Perhaps the brain creates processing cycles in which cues are retrieved and tested.[69] When many traces or associates are associated with a given cue, at least one of them is likely to come out early on.

The prototypes of letters may be created through statistical averages that people compute on the basis of the figures they have seen many times.[70] As a result, a "good," simple figure of each letter is formed in the brain (referring to the principle called *pragnanz*). To learn the prototype, consistency may initially be helpful. To find a matching prototype and recognize an image, according to one theory, the image of an object may first be analyzed and broken down to basic geometric components, such as blocks, cylinders, wedges, or cones (called *geons*).[71] Just by perceiving two or three geons of an image, people are able to see a whole and recognize entire objects, even if they are displayed for very brief periods of time (such as a stylized picture of a horse) flashed for 100 milliseconds. This may be the reason why expert readers recognize full words and letters even if only the upper or lower half is exposed. Automatic readers know the "good" prototypical letter forms and have a sense of how much it is possible to distort them before they morph into other letters or become unrecognizable.

Various letter combinations (and their critical features or individual geons) may be organized in the brain on the basis of innate perceptual rules, called *gestalt*. According to these rules, similar items, familiar items, or items near each other are grouped together. Series of dots are seen as forming in straight or smoothly curving lines, and the lines tend to be seen as following the smoothest path. Open circles may be seen as closed, and symmetrically located items are also seen as pertaining to the same pattern. Letters and words are seen as having boundaries, and the boundaries of two letters usually do not get confused, nor are the letters of two neighboring words usually mixed up.[72]

The matching processes happen very fast, within milliseconds.[73] The time frame within which the visual signals are presented and processed matters and if too many features are presented too fast, some brains may be unable to process them in the order and rhythm they come. Certain brain areas may function as a spell checker, and reading problems may arise if letter patterns arrive a few milliseconds too slowly to be checked as a whole.[74]

The letters in the various scripts have developed over hundreds of years to be distinguishable by relatively accomplished readers.[75] Though many letters have similar strokes, they have also acquired features to make distinction possible.[76] Similar letters may be written higher or lower than others, have dots, connect or not connect to other letters, have similar components of different sizes or be set at different angles. Even scripts that are difficult to decode phonologically, such as Arabic, have survived over the centuries because enough people learn to identify quickly enough the critical differences among letters. However, these differences are often minute, and a small change in an angle or ratio of lines may make a different letter.[77] Initially, distinction may be difficult. The learner must learn which features are critical, shift attention to them and decrease attention to others, detect specialized parts of letters, make minute differentiations among similar features, and eventually see the individual features as parts of larger units that form the basis of large-scale automatic recognition of text.[78] How is that possible?

## Brain Capacity for Perceptual Learning

With training, learners shift from perceiving stimuli grossly to making very fine discriminations among various categories and functions. It helps if the memory is "primed" by a symbol (for example, that letters are capitalized), and then a person knows which distinction rules must used on that occasion.[79] For example, with a few days of training it is possible to recognize camouflaged moths on trees, discern vague faces, or see the sex of chickens. With practice, the accuracy improves dramatically, and recognition takes very little time, for example, dropping from 130 msec to 30 msec over several days. Learning fine discrimination helps see patterns holistically. Thus, within a few days, people may learn to identify multiple targets simultaneously. In one experiment, researchers trained people to identify photos of 10 unfamiliar human faces embedded in varying degrees of visual camouflage resembling the black and white static on an untuned TV. After several days, performance improved by up to 400 percent and people were able to identify faces that were nearly invisible to them at the start of training. To see if this improvement was caused by a reduction in the brain's variability, the researchers presented the same sequence of patterns again and measured response consistency. They found the consistent responses and also found that improvements are enduring. Like automatic reading, once people learn the recognition features, they do not forget them. However, learning is highly specific to the visual figures encountered during training. When people get better at distinguishing a vertical line from one that is slightly tilted, improvement does not transfer to other orientations, such as a horizontal line.[80] Research shows that perceptual training has enduring results, and people do not easily forget it.

Perceptual learning rules give some insights into the most effective ways to present letter patterns to learners. Training with easy discriminations first allows people to give attention to the relevant dimension. People discriminate better if they are told the dimensions, so they should be told what differentiates one letter from another.[81] People are better able to distinguish between stimuli that come from different categories than when they come from the same category. Thus, the Latin letters p, q, b, and d may be seen in one category of circle-and-vertical line and more similar to each other than to x. So, differences between categories of letter shapes may be emphasized in training. Performance may also improve when learners understand which dimensions are irrelevant, that is, that a "serif" under the q does not change the letter. They easily learn to detect features and expect accents, or a dot over the Latin i. They can also learn how letter patterns are located in space, for example, above or below the line, or as in Arabic, identify letters despite variable length or downward sloping.[82] Minute differentiation includes deciphering people's handwriting. However, discrimination training is highly specific to the targets used and does not often transfer from one type of letter or line to another.[83] For example, learning to read through one type font does not easily transfer to other type fonts or calligraphic letters.[84]

Perceptual learning is to some extent biologically determined, and some of its aspects may be affected by critical periods of development. Though neural plasticity certainly exists throughout life, many of the most dramatic changes to human perceptual systems occur within the first seven years of life, and change may not be easy later. Several studies have found that a few exposures to a word may be sufficient for a child to acquire word-specific orthographic information,[85] but perhaps adults need longer. Perceptual dimensions that are easily isolated by adults are treated as fused by children; thus, children cannot easily access the individual dimensions that compose an object.[86] Perhaps inability to perceive individual dimensions may somehow facilitate encapsulation and automatic recognition of words for children. Perhaps children can also connect sound to the encapsulated (or unitized) objects that they see more easily than adults.

### *Implications for Instruction*
### **Perceptual Learning**

Perceptual learning could offer considerable help in making literacy acquisition more efficient. However, perceptual research does not often use letters as stimuli, since they are well-known in industrialized countries. Some suggestions from the current state of knowledge are:

- Letters could be presented in literacy classes and textbooks in sequences that would help detection of critical features and discrimination of minute details such as the number of dots on Arabic letters. To enable focusing on the correct dimensions, letters should initially be of the same type font. Also, letter or word patterns must be consistently linked to specific sounds or concepts. But in later lessons, various type fonts could be introduced, including handwriting. Discrimination training could progress from easy to hard, initially avoiding teaching together the letters that look similar, but eventually juxtaposing them, after learners have connected them frequently to sounds and seen them inside words.
- Learners in specific scripts could be surveyed to find out which letters they confuse or take longer to identify. Then they could be asked over several days to find these letters in sheets of

# Cognitive Science in the Service of Adult Literacy

letters as fast as they can. The task can be gradually made more complex and include multiple letter searches. Newspapers could be used, thus making the task more relevant to actual reading use.[87] If computers become available to literacy classes, this exercise may also be programmed.

- Letters shaped differently from others (such as Latin X, Arabic k, or Hindi ksh) stand out and their sounds are rapidly identified. To a beginning reader who reads serially most of the time, these may be learned faster and may be easier to locate in an array of letters, such as I's or T's, that have vertical lines. Salient letters may be processed in parallel with the less distinguishable letters. Perhaps such salient letters can be introduced in textbooks and instruction and interspersed in such a way as to facilitate reading of other letters. People who still read serially may use such salient letters to search for words in texts or dictionaries that they otherwise do not recognize automatically.

- To facilitate encapsulation and perception of entire words as a unit, the space or print contrast could be increased between successive words, particularly those that are confusing.[88] Connecting letters may also be useful for scripts that can connect letters.

- *Kinesthetic learning may transfer to visual recognition.* Perceptual training often transfers not just within a sensory modality but across sensory modalities;[89] so it is possible for touch to help with visual recognition. Tracing letters on a hand should reinforce reading. It may facilitate the memorization of confusing letters, such as p, q, b, d, which, if rotated, give different sounds. Other literacy practitioners have also underlined the importance of kinesthetic features involved in tracing and advocate tracing letters by finger on a rough surface while repeating the sound.[90] This treatment is used extensively for the brain damage type called alexia (see below). Tracing letters is an old idea, but it has not been used systematically.

- *Writing is important but neglected.* Reading and writing are not parallel functions, and it is possible for one to lag behind the other.[91] In the limited time of literacy instruction, writing often has a lower priority. Some practitioners believe that the simultaneous teaching of reading and writing may slow the acquisition of both, and production of text by learners is time-consuming. It may be more effective to focus on building fluency in reading and then moving to writing.[92] Yet, writing may facilitate perceptual learning; significant motor and visuospatial abilities are reinforced through copying during basic reading instruction.[93] Furthermore, it may help reading skills to be retained longer. (See below.)

The literature still says little about how to connect letters to sounds most efficiently. If a letter shape is distinct, for some reason, its sound may be more likely to be retained. Pattern discrimination may be learned eventually and not forgotten, but the connection of the pattern with the sound is less stable. Often, people who relapse into illiteracy remember the visual patterns but cannot assign sound values to them.

## Beginning Readers of Various Scripts: Putting it All Together

What do beginning adult readers of various scripts face? They read serially and slowly, learning to discriminate among letters and apply decoding rules at the same time. Letter complexes may change pronunciation according to position, and the reader must decide early on how to pronounce a word. Some scripts, such as Latin, Greek, Cyrillic, and Armenian, are easier because they consist of letters presented in a single line, though all have some diphthongs that must be pronounced together. When the Latin script is used in languages that match sounds exactly and predictably to letter combinations (such as Spanish, Italian, and most recently, written languages in Africa or Asia), semi-skilled readers can decode the messages quite easily.[94] Consequently, even one month of literacy class was found to produce measurable skills in Mexico and Serbia, where a literate environment also facilitates practice.[95] Decoding of serially written scripts may be more difficult in languages where letter pronunciation changes according to some rules (such as Malagache and Russian vowels, French endings, Greek diphthongs). Reading serially is notoriously difficult for languages that use the Latin letters rather unpredictably, like Dutch and English. Readers must recognize simultaneously most letters of a word to pronounce it.

Even when sounds correspond clearly to specific letters, certain scripts require parallel processing or unitized perception and fine discrimination early on in a literacy class. The syllabic scripts of India have superscripts and subscripts to represent vowels and other sounds; the reader must read above and below a letter simultaneously in order to decode the pattern correctly. Furthermore, detailed pattern discrimination must take place above the consonant line, where vowels, nasals, and r sounds may mix. If readers skip any of these signs or read them in an incorrect order, they read the words wrong. Indian languages have various complexities. For example, Bangla requires the reader to process three signs in a row simultaneously to form a consonant and the vowel o; for example,.the combination "ko" as shown below:

কো

If the first two signs are read without the third, which is really an a, the combination will be read as "ke"

কে

instead of "ko." For example, "Jomi" is given as

জোমি

Predictably, this letter complex poses difficulties for Bengali neoliterates. Similarly, Hindi readers must read back and forth if they read serially words such as '"vargon 'ko" (to groups), where the r and the n become part of next vowel complex as given below:

वर्गों को

Many literacy class participants incorrectly read or skip the superscripts and subscripts as they process letters serially.

### Forgetting—Relapse into Illiteracy

When governments and donors finance literacy programs, they do so with the expectation that once made literate, people will stay literate. However, that expectation holds true only if reading functions have been largely automatized. If people must make conscious decisions about the letters and words they see, their reading skills may be forgotten, particularly if they are not used often. Thus, it should not be surprising that at least some neoliterates lapse back into illiteracy. The frequent calls for post-literacy suggest that reading skills acquired in literacy classes may not be automatized and may decay if not reinforced.

How soon and by how much are skills likely to decay? Surprisingly, relapse into illiteracy has been researched very little, and findings are contradictory. Some literacy programs show considerable relapse (47 percent in a Nepalese program), while others show very little (a Ugandan program).[96] The amount of prior proficiency is often unknown, so a clear answer is hard to get. However, forgetting rates of various skills have been studied since the nineteenth century, and general inferences are possible.

Literacy involves several skills: learning of procedures, reactions to visual stimuli, and writing (psychomotor skills).[97] These types of skills are forgotten at different rates. Information and procedural skills have been researched extensively, and they involve rapid forgetting; research on

## Box 1. Arabic: A Very Difficult Script for Adult Learners

To have enough time in working memory for accessing the context of the words and comprehending the message, letter recognition must be extremely fast. What happens when a script requires decisions on word meanings while the reader still decodes slowly?

The Arabic script was originally developed for a Semitic language, in which vowels are predictable from the consonant configurations. Its use spread to Indo-European languages, such as Urdu, Persian, Pashtu, and Kurdish, and in earlier years to others as well (such as Shikomori of the Comoros islands, Bahasa Indonesia, Wolof, Pulaar, and Ottoman Turkish). All these languages have unpredictable vowels and need to differentiate between e, i, o, u. Minor adjustments have been made to consonants, but vowels are usually written according to Arabic conventions. Thus, in daily writing, only consonants and the existence of long vowels are indicated; short vowels (for which special signs exist) and the exact pronunciation of long vowels are omitted, and it is impossible to differentiate between a and e, o and u.

In all languages, the Arabic letters only approximately represent the sounds. In effect, one needs to know the meaning of a word before one can read it. It is, therefore, impossible to read words letter by letter. Readers must scan a whole sentence, go through more grammar decoding, and employ guessing strategies before arriving at the correct interpretation of the words. This places considerable stress on the working memory, which must hold all the alternatives while decisions are made about the meaning of the text. The script also presents perceptual challenges. The letters are connected, and the reader must be trained in minute spatial discriminations through relative placements and distances of dots. Handwritten Arabic is often written with a downward slant, with some letters on top of others. All these processing problems present special challenges for adult neoliterates.[98] Some examples of confusion are:

| | | | |
|---|---|---|---|
| نخِّ | nakhla – palm tree | she was (kanat) | كنت |
| نحِّ | nahla – bee | was (kuntu) | كنت |
| نجِّ | najla – daughter | flag ('alam) | علم |
| | | knowledge ('ilm) | علم |
| | | the flag, the knowledge (al 'alam) | العلم |

The script only has about 22 letters, and it is easily taught to children in Koranic schools; curiously, most learn to perceive the intricate and non-linear word patterns in a few months and read without comprehension, though they often come up with the wrong word alternatives. However, reading problems are widespread among Arab children, who find it difficult to develop reading comprehension or read reliably without vowels for several years. In addition, the Arabic script is used only to render standard Arabic, and does not reliably render dialects (like those of Morocco and Tunisia) that change vowel values. These dialects remain essentially unwritten, and to write letters, people often resort to French. As a result of reading problems, poverty, and women's limited access to education, illiteracy in Arabic-speaking countries is among the highest in the world, 56.5 percent in 1996.[99]

*Source:* Author's data.

U.S. Army reservists showed that knowledge about army jobs and procedures decayed within six months.[100] Psychomotor skills decay at a slower rate. For example, the weapons qualifications of U.S. Army reservists did not begin to decay until 10 months had passed. Also, people who start learning a skill from zero find it harder to retain than people who are improving already existing knowledge. Thus, the previous skill qualification score was the best predictor of skill retention for Army reservists, followed by an aptitude score.

From the available research it can be concluded that:

- The skills of unschooled adults who rarely use them (for example, those who live in rural areas) can be forgotten substantially. The model shown in Figure 5 suggests that about 50 percent of the reading skill may be forgotten within six months of training.[101] Since the focus of reading is words and comprehension, forgetting half the letters (if that is the case) would render someone unable to read.
- Writing may not be forgotten as easily. Thus, extensive writing (more than is currently used in literacy courses) might in some ways protect against skills loss. (Perhaps the extensive copying that children do in low-income countries that lack textbooks consolidates their memory of letter shapes, even if they do not remember how to connect them into words.)

## Figure 5. A Forgetting Curve of Procedural Knowledge

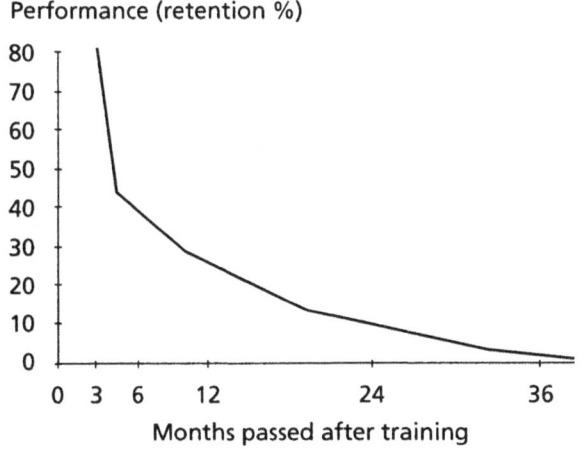

*Source:* Adapted from McKenna and Glendon (1985) – Forgetting of trainees of cardiopulmonary resuscitation techniques

- Learners who have been to school before and know a little reading are more likely to retain the knowledge imparted in a literacy class. This variable may account for the contradictory findings regarding relapse into illiteracy. In a Uganda program, where relapse was minimal,[102] about 75 percent of the learners had been to school for an average of four years. In a Bangladesh program, where two samples showed that only 32–34 percent could still read, most participants had been unschooled.[103]
- The amount of time spent learning and opportunities to elaborate information increase the probability that reading will be retained. The existing research on relapse indicates that skills were forgotten more often in rural areas (where opportunities to practice are fewer) and poor-quality schools.[104] Indeed, desultory literacy instruction may fail to make people literate, and subsequent assessment attributes the low outcomes to relapse.[105]

Observations suggest that what is mainly forgotten is the connection of letters with the sound, not the shape of the letters.[106] People typically remember that they have seen a letter, but they forget its sound. Contemporary theories of forgetting focus on interference or the inaccessibility of a memory given disuse rather than plain decay of information.[107] It is also known that retrieval is a potent event, more important than studying again previously learned material. The more difficult and involved the retrieval, the better the item is registered in memory thereafter.[108] However, it is unknown how the multiple skills involved in literacy are forgotten and why or how the order of letters taught affects their probability of being remembered when seen infrequently. Given the cost and expectations of literacy programs, this should be a priority area of research.

### *Implications for Instruction*
### *Forgetting*

> Forgetting should be expected during and after the course, particularly if readers do not acquire automaticity. This issue should become an important topic of teacher training.
>
> Until more research is available, the best recommendation is to remind learners to practice often after the end of the course and try hard to remember what they learned. Retrieving material previously learned makes it more likely to be retained in the long term.
>
> Mnemonics about letters might be helpful in recalling sounds when the memory about specific letters becomes inaccessible. They may create more stable connections if learners themselves make them up according to their existing knowledge.

## The Reading Difficulties of Adult Learners

*All I see is a jumble of letters ... I know them all but I don't see words.*[109]

Between 1992 and 2001, the author observed many nonformal as well as children's formal classes during World Bank supervision or evaluation missions. The differences between the reading performance of adults and children were striking. Children from very poor backgrounds in the schools of the Bangladeshi NGO Gono Shahaja Shangstha were reading the rather complex Bangla script fast and fluently in the middle of grade 2. Second graders who had attended madrasas of the Comoros islands were able to write Shikomori in the Arabic script and read it fluently from the blackboard, though they could hardly read French in school, which they did not understand. Burkinabé children at the end of first grade of the Nomgana bilingual program read fluently school texts in Mooré, while Chilean first graders of low-income schools read texts fluently by the middle of the first grade. When languages have simple decoding rules and children receive sufficient instruction, most read fluently by the end of grade one.[110]

By contrast, adults in literacy classes read with effort, haltingly, spending time on specific letters. They make mistakes often. When they read aloud, their intonation often indicates limited or no understanding of the text. They may only fit 2–3 words in their working memory span and seem to be stuck in the decoding stage of reading.[111] Learners may decode small chunks of two or three letters simultaneously, but not words, particularly longer words.[112] Somehow, the links between symbols and their underlying codes are fragile. Connections between letters and sounds are tenuous and easily forgotten.

More systematic observations took place during Swiss-financed literacy research in Burkina Faso in 2000–01 (Annex A). The classes catered to all village illiterates, so teenagers and adults were mixed. Some adults noticed that after a few weeks, younger teenagers read faster. When teachers presented reading cards to the whole class, the teenage students were the first to decode them. Adults did not volunteer to read as often as the teenage learners. Sometimes the researchers created age groups to enhance participation from adults. It was even considered opportune to split classes of many ages into age groups and do different activities in order to avoid embarrassment to older people.[113]

Though age statistics are rarely mentioned in documents, observations indicate that literacy class participants are mainly adolescents and young adults. Relatively few people in their 30s, 40s or older attend. For example, the average age of participants in a Kenyan program that was studied ethnologically was 23, although the group had some 50- and 60-year olds.[114] The mean age of Burkinabé learners in the Swiss-financed literacy study was 20 (Annex A). Certainly, adults may fail to enroll or stay in classes for social and economic reasons. However, little research has been done to compare the reading achievement of children and adults given the same instructional amount of time, amount of homework, and similar materials.[115]

The unschooled are not the only people who have reading difficulties. Additional evidence comes from the *problems of educated adults fluent in foreign languages that use scripts different from the script of their native language*. Readers who become literate in one script can learn rapidly the letter shapes and rules of another script, since they have phonological awareness and understanding of decoding strategies.[116] However, skill in discriminating one set of patterns does not transfer to another. These readers read slowly, have difficulty perceiving letters in groups, depend on sound to understand words, make many errors, tend to forget quickly, and have difficulty in reading artistic letters. Interview information suggests that foreign readers need to look at words for longer periods, just like beginning readers. They may not process the letters in the short eye fixation times employed for the scripts they learned as children. This was reported even for scripts that share many letters with Latin, such as Greek and Russian. Highly educated professionals who continually use scripts learned in adulthood report that reading difficulties persist for decades. The author has yet to meet an expert reader of a script learned in adulthood.[117] But the problem has not been clearly identified or researched, because poor reading is confounded with lack of reading practice and low levels of language fluency.[118]

Does age cause difficulties in some functions that help automatize reading? This is possible, because children perform differently than adults in some aspects of perceptual learning. Since perceptual research has not focused on literacy acquisition, important questions remain unanswered. Studies do exist on the ability to make fast decisions with respect to visual displays and indicate slower decisions with age; however, they compare young people to the elderly and are not suitable paradigms for literacy.[119] A somewhat more relevant paradigm is air traffic controller training, which demands rapid processing of visual and spatial information. Increased age has been found to be negatively related to probability of success, particularly after age 35.[120]

Perhaps, one or more of the tasks that determine reading automaticity have a critical period, and automaticity may be hard to acquire after this period is over.[121] Developmental psychology provides some support. Some reading specialists in the United States have found that if children do not learn to read early in their primary school careers, they will not learn to read well later. Intervention is effective in the first one or two years of school, but learning to read after age 15 becomes quite difficult.[122] Maturation, particularly with the onset of puberty, brings about tremendous change in the brains of schooled children. Tasks that involve speed become harder to master after puberty, and the ability to learn languages from the environment is also severely curtailed.[123] Perhaps it becomes harder to attach symbols to the brain's dictionary of meanings as age increases, whether these symbols are visual or auditory.

## Health Issues Affecting Reading Performance

Because reading involves many brain functions, it is influenced by a person's mental abilities.[124] People with borderline retardation are often weak readers. Participants in literacy classes may suffer from cognitive deficiencies as a result of young maternal age, difficult births, low birth weight (particularly for girls[125]), repeated giardia infections,[126] violence,[127] exposure to toxins, anemia, or malnutrition.[128] Iodine deficiency occurs in many areas of heavy rainfall (as in Bangladesh) and is associated with reduced intelligence, psychomotor retardation, impaired hearing, and mental and neurological damage. Also, protein-energy malnutrition affects the cognitive functions of girls in particular, such as the ability to learn categories, to process and structure information, to learn and react to social and environmental cues, to ask appropriate questions within a given environment, and to identify and solve relevant problems. Such problems may account to some extent for the poor learning outcomes of formal and nonformal classes.

Reading difficulties may also be due to dyslexia. Dyslexics read haltingly, have poor short-term memory for verbal sounds, and have difficulty becoming automatic readers.[129] Disruption in their neural systems is evident at a preschool age.[130] But the deficits of dyslexics are not only linguistic, they are also auditory and visual.[131] About 5–15 percent of U.S. children are affected with dyslexia, and apparently, the English spelling may cause problems to susceptible people. Dyslexia reportedly manifests itself half as often among Italians who must learn simple spelling rules, than among British children, even when scans show dyslexic brain patterns.[132] One would suppose a lower frequency of dyslexia in countries that have largely phonetic writing systems. However, the health factors associated with limited cognitive development are much more prevalent in poor countries, and their burden may outweigh the benefits of an easy script. It is possible, therefore, that there are more problem readers in the classrooms of poorer countries than previously believed, and possibly more in poor English-speaking countries (such as Trinidad and Jamaica) or in countries that extensively make young children literate through

English (such as Uganda, Kenya, and Ghana) or French (Francophone Africa).

Possible treatments for dyslexia have been researched extensively, and the findings may help improve the reading skills of adult neoliterates. English-speaking dyslexics can read better through techniques that help pull out the sounds of words they try to read. For example, an eight-week program resulted in measurable improvement in reading scores and changes in brain scans. Training produced increased activity in the left stem of the brain where language is processed, but also compensatory changes in the right hemisphere. Just as some stroke victims shift functions to the undamaged side of their brain, so can people trying to make up for the loss of function with a disorder like dyslexia.[133] Dyslexics who have a dysfunction of the general sensory system may benefit from training that involves sound distinctions. Finnish researchers found that a computer game based on patterns and sounds not only improved reading skills among 7 year olds with dyslexia, but also spurred measurable changes in the children's brain activity.[134] These and other methods might have broader use for adult illiterates if they are found to be effective and technologically sustainable.[135]

Certain types of brain damage create *alexia*, a condition involving loss of connections between the visual cortex and the angular gyrus, where many reading functions reside. People with this condition lose the ability to read automatically; they revert to reading letter by letter, need much longer to identify long words, and make errors recognizing letters, confusing visually similar letters for one another. People with alexia have benefited from a tactile-kinesthetic strategy to improve accuracy.[136] They use their fingers to trace large models of letters, then they look at the letters and trace them with a pencil on their free palm while naming them. The tactile input to the hand helps identify the letters.

Overall, what factors can cause reading problems for adult learners?

- *Cognition.* Areas of low cognitive performance may be interfering with the acquisition of fluent reading. The working memory of the unschooled may simply be too short for the needs of reading. A short working memory may affect in particular the more memory-demanding scripts like Arabic.[137] On the other hand, the illiterates' phonological and semantic processors seem to work well. Learners attempt to find suitable words and often rely on context and make up words after having read just one or two letters.
- *Perceptual learning.* Clearly perceptual learning has age-related issues. Apparently, adults can rapidly discriminate between letters of various shapes; letters that look different or take more space (like the initial Arabic k) stand out and are identified more easily. However, adults

have difficulty in identifying handwriting or artistic letters (Figure 6). This raises the possibility that the pragnanz principle is not applied well, and that adults may not form "good," prototypical figures of some letters. Perhaps the memory does not save some copies of variations or does not retrieve them as efficiently as with children to compare to presented letters. Perhaps adults have some difficulty in learning to detect critical features in letters and disregard irrelevant ones. Without this ability, and the ability to identify patterns in changing space, it may not be easy to decipher connected letters (as in typical Arabic print or English handwriting) after having learned their separate counterparts. Superscripts and subscripts in scripts like Hindi should be perceived as linked to the letters that have them, but adults tend to see them separately and misread them. Multiple overlapping lines (as in superscript combinations of Hindi and Bangla) are not easily disentangled.
- *Connections to sound and integration of functions.* A difficulty may also exist in the interpretation of the perceived patterns in connection with assigned sounds.[138] Some connections among various parts of the brain may function less well for adults (as in alexia).

Perhaps a combination of difficulties exists, exacerbated also by health factors. But the result is that learners may need more time and exposure than children to automatize reading, and they may not get sufficient practice in literacy classes (particularly given the limited time these teach reading effectively). After finishing the courses, they may have limited opportunities to see variations of letters and develop stable mental pictures of them. However, it is unknown how much practice is needed by adult learners of various scripts and languages to reach automaticity.

## Figure 6. Differences in Printed and Handwritten Letters May Confuse Neoliterates

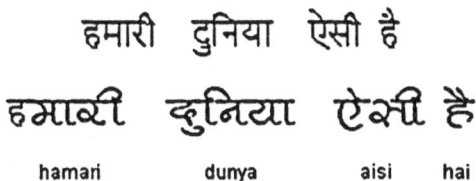

hamari     dunya     aisi     hai

Hindi: "Our world is like this."

*Source:* Author's data.

Sometimes learners themselves are disappointed and discouraged by the limited skills they acquire; and this may be one reason for the significant dropout of many programs. But difficulties may not be insurmountable. Perhaps adults need a much larger number of trials than children in pairing letters with sounds as well as specific perceptual learning exercises to become automatic. The issue is how to put such methods in place in the literacy classes of the poor. To put their brains to work, learners must have opportunities to obtain information. However, an important problem is that *instruction may be ineffective or infrequent, so learners may not learn much that they can later remember.* The next section discusses these issues.

## Notes

1. Functional magnetic resonance imaging, which enables the brain metabolism to be studied during various tasks. Other techniques include positron emission tomography (PET), which involves injection of radioactive dyes and can only be given to subjects once a year, magnetoencephalography (MEG), magnetic source imaging (MSI), and evoked potentials, which monitor brain arousal in response to various stimuli and inform on the temporal characteristics of signal processing (Sekuler and Blake 2001, p. 23).

2. Thanks are due to: James Mike Royer, University of Massachusetts at Amherst, U.S.; Richard Venezky, University of Delaware, U.S.; Virginia Berninger, University of Washington, U.S.; John Sabatini and Mohammad Maamouri, University of Pennsylvania, U.S.; Robert Sekuler, Brandeis University, U.S.; Michael Merzenich, University of California at San Francisco, U.S.; Irving Biederman, University of Southern California, Los Angeles, U.S.; Alan Baddeley, University of Bristol, UK; Karl Magnus Petersson, Karolinska Hospital, Stockholm, Sweden; Alexandra Reis, Universidade do Algarve, Faro, Portugal; Vijayalakshmi Rabindranath, National Brain Research Center, Delhi, India; Alfredo Ardila, Miami Institute of Psychology, U.S.; Alison Sekuler, McMaster University, Canada; Rhonda Friedman, Georgetown University, U.S.; Robert Goldstone, Indiana University, Bloomington, U.S.; Hugh Miller, Nottinham Trent University, Nottinham, UK; Robert Bjork, University of California, Los Angeles, U.S..

3. Godwin 2001.

4. Varney 2002. Findings suggest that the ancient skills of gesture comprehension and animal tracking were the underpinnings of brain organization that permitted reading to occur.

5. Words and pseudowords produce prominent responses along the inner surface of the left cerebral hemisphere (Posner & Raichle 1997, p. 78–81). Phonological processing (getting the sound of words from letters) and decoding involve the regions around the planum temporale and the inferior parietal lobe. Interpreting

language involves several temporal, parietal, and prefrontal regions encompassing a large part of the language-dominant hemisphere.

6. For example, London taxi drivers were found to have a larger hippocampus, which is involved in short-term memory and spatial memory (Maguire et al. 1997).

7. Research by Jay Giedd (National Institute of Mental Health, Bethesda, Maryland) reported in Begley 2000.

8. In Levi 1996. Luria deduced that illiterates could not reason abstractly and has been criticized for cultural insensitivity, but Lecours (1989) made similar observations. The localized activation shown in brain scans of illiterates may lend some support to these observations.

9. Laboratory of Comparative Human Cognition 1986.

10. Reis et al. 2001.

11. However, language has a balanced representation between the two hemispheres in literates and illiterates. The superior parts of the angular-supramarginal regions seem more active on the left than on the right hemisphere in illiterate subjects, whereas the reverse may be the case for the inferior parts and the precuneus. (Alexandra Reis, personal communication, April 2002.)

12. Petersson et al. 2001; Ardila et al. 2000a, using neuropsychological tasks.

13. Reis and Castro-Caldas 1997; Castro-Caldas et al. 1998.

14. Comings et al. 1998. Some early references were made regarding listening in Gray (1953) also Dexter et al. (1998). Morais et al. (1987) found that Portuguese illiterates performed worse than literates, when asked to identify different words coming simultaneously in each ear (dichotically). Literates may focus on the phonemic constituents of speech, thus recognizing ambiguous speech more effectively.

15. Reis et al. 2001.

16. Ardila et al. 1989; Ardila et al. 2000a; Reis et al. 2001.

17. Ardila and Rosselli 1989. A subsystem of the working memory, called the phonological loop, stores sound patterns while more permanent memory records are being constructed, possibly for language-learning purposes (Baddeley 1999). Schooling may train it, but if it does not function well, children have difficulty reading. Poor readers generally do not perform well in short-term memory tasks, such as digit span, serial recall of unrelated strings of words, and the repetition of artificial words. However, it is unclear how illiterates process digits in their memory, whether by size, shape, or magnitude. Thus, these tasks may not be measuring verbal memory after all.

18. Ostrosky et al. 1998; Ardila et al. 2000b.

19. Ardila et al. 2000a; Instituto Nacional de Educación para los Adultos 1998.

20. Riddell 2001. Beginning from visual cards, illiterates gradually build on key words on these maps or matrices. Basic syllables are introduced, then several words and phrases are added. As the learning units proceed, the facilitators stress the "active" process of learner's writing rather than the "passive" process of reading.

21. Seidenberg and McClelland 1989.

22. Readers in some languages (such as Bangla) have developed reading rules that beginners learn by heart and recite as they try to read (for example, j + a = ja).

23. For automaticity acquisition in Braille and Morse code see Brunner and Brunner (1968).

24. Sekuler and Blake 2001, p. 254.

25. Brain imaging studies show that areas involved in processing words and linguistically correct pseudowords are separate from brain areas used to process consonant strings and non-letters (Venezky 2001).

26. Reicher 1969; Wheeler 1970.

27. The word superiority effect may be one reason why children who learn to read in languages they do not know face obstacles. If they do not know the meaning of many words in the textbooks, they will see few words they can identify and thus be deprived of the letter-level reinforcement that they would receive from known words.

28. Hook and Jones 2002.

29. Silent reading norms are: Second grade 60–100 words per minute, third grade 90–120, fourth grade 110–140, fifth grade 140–170, and six grade 160–190 words per minute. (Barr et al. 2002, p. 76). Oral reading norm for grade 1 is 30–70 words per minute. For an extensive review of literacy acquisition basics, see Venezky 2001.

30. Hook and Jones 2002.

31. Regardless of spelling regularity, research indicates that mastering the alphabetic principle is essential to reading proficiency, and methods that teach it are more effective than methods that do not (Rayner et al. 2001).

32. Saldanha 2000, 1999.

33. Explanations and examples are provided at Web sites, such as http://www.readuk.com/phonographix.html or http://learningconnectionsinc.com/programs.htm.

34. Word lengths differ in various languages. Grammatically simpler sentences may require less effort to read, so this estimate is rather rough.

35. According to Barr et al. (2002, p. 253) reading performance levels on the basis of accuracy in the United States are: Independent reading (98–100% accuracy), instructional (95–97% accuracy, can function with guidance), borderline (90–94% accuracy, struggles to sound out words, comprehension difficult), frustration (90% accuracy or less, functions inadequately, uncomfortable with reading). At the "borderline" accuracy level, only about 50–74% comprehension questions can be answered correctly. Also see Betts (1954) and the Eritrea National Reading Survey (2002).

36. Barr et al. 2002, p. 76

37. The relationship between reading and working memory is not well understood. At least in children, reading may also help lengthen the working memory. Illiterates may perform worse in working memory tasks due to difficulty with

more fine-grained sublexical representations (Alexandra Reis, personal communication, April 2002).

38. Limage 1999; UNESCO Statistical Yearbook 1999–2000.
39. Torres 2001.
40. Comings et al. undated.
41. Because automatic skills are not forgotten, they cannot easily be set aside when no longer needed. For example, the movements involved in smoking are a major obstacle in quitting. Many drivers find it very difficult to drive on the other side of the road when changing countries.
42. Experiments to define automatized skills include matching letters with numbers and then studying the reaction time of subjects as they practice the associations between the two and recall one from the other. For such simple tasks, automaticity is achieved after 10–30 presentations. However, learning to reading with automaticity includes larger numbers of stimuli than tested with these experiments as well as interpretation of texts.
43. Stroop 1935.
44. For example, in a memory search task in which random digits would appear on a screen, trained subjects were as fast in judging whether a digit was one of the four "target" digits—for example, 1, 4, 7, or 8—as they were when the target set consisted of only one digit. In a perceptual task in which various numbers of digits were shown on the screen simultaneously, the time they took to judge whether a target digit was on display was independent of the number of digits shown displayed (Irving Biederman, personal communication, February 2002).
45. The technique of evoked potentials is also appropriate; it shows limited and brief arousal of the cerebral cortex to an automatically processed stimulus, such as a street sign. This technique relates perceptual judgments made in response to a given stimulus to the electrical brain activity evoked by that same stimulus through electrodes attached to the scalp (Sekuler and Blake 2001, p. 23).
46. Researchers have studied the principles of serial processing by asking subjects to find a T or an I in an array of letters that have similar strokes. In a serial search, each item in an array must be attended to and a decision must be made about it (such as whether the letter is a T or an I) before moving on to each subsequent item. In this mode, reaction and recognition time will increase with the addition of each new stimulus. By contrast, in a parallel search the entire area of a display is scanned simultaneously until the target is spotted. It was found that if the displays of experimental stimuli are small, processing occurs serially, but as the size increases, search time eventually levels off, indicating parallel search processes (Treisman and Gelade 1980).
47. Transition to automaticity occurs in four stages: (a) initial processing of items one by one, bringing them consciously to memory; (b) a combination of controlled and automatic processing; (c) principally automatic processing with controlled processing assisting; and (d) completely automatic processing. With practice, processing changes from completely controlled to a mixture or

controlled and automatic, to completely autonomous (Schneider 1986; Logan et al. 1996; Logan and Klapp 1991).

48. Computerized neural network models, such as the interactive activation model by J.L. McClelland, have been created to understand how a reader processes information. This area is beyond the topic of this paper.

49. On the other hand, the act of reading aloud, as often required in religious instruction, may detract from the extraction of meaning because some of the attention is spent on producing correct sounds. Even skilled readers may find it difficult to understand a moderately difficult passage that they read aloud.

50. Royer 1997.

51. Words presented at the same place on computer screens considerably diminish the need for eyes to move and may speed up reading; reducing eye movement may save beginning readers' time in the working memory span.

52. Apparently, an application exists in South Africa (Lauglo 2001, p. 40).

53. Examples are the Simputer, an inexpensive, Indian-made computer for people of limited literacy, and Leapfrog, an electronic reader and speaker in various languages targeted towards children (www.leapfrog.com). To enable multiple trials and overlearning of units of various lengths, the author developed the prototype of a multilingual computer tutorial through a Swiss Trust fund grant. The software enables learners to hear the sounds of letters, combinations, words, and sentences. The stimuli are presented in timed intervals, ranging from a few seconds to 250 milliseconds. Readers' reaction times are stored for monitoring and data analysis purposes. To facilitate generalization beyond the most standard letter forms, various fonts may be used, including those that imitate handwriting. In the prototype, the language content can be entered by teachers in the Latin and Hindi scripts.

54. Rayner et al. 2001.

55. Ancient Greek inscriptions typically have no spaces between words, suggesting that perhaps the writers did not have good phonological awareness. Also, earlier Greek inscriptions (for example, from the eigth to sixth century BC) are written by starting left to right on one line and continuing right to left on the next (boustrophedon), suggesting that readers processed them serially. The eventual standardization of writing in specific directions and word formation may indicate that their writers had achieved parallel processing and automaticity.

56. Stanovich 1988, 1993–94; Gathercole and Baddeley 1993; National Reading Panel 2000.

57. Durgunoglu and Oney 1999.

58. Guessing from context is a poor way to read, and the readers who mainly rely on context are weak. Poor readers also do not monitor their reading as well as good readers (Venezky et al. 1998.)

59. Morais et al. 1988.

60. Gombert 1994.

61. Bertelson et al. 1989.

62. Morais et al. 1979.

63. Morais et al. 1988.

64. Hanley et al. 1999. Chinese adults who were taught literacy through ideograms did not improve in phonological awareness skills, whereas those taught through the Latin-based phonetic script Pinyin did (Read et al. 1984).

65. Rayner et al. 2001.

66. Solan et al. 1995. The authors tested movement through Eye-track, an infrared eye movement recording device.

67. Coltheart 1978. The dual route theory proposes two possible routes to provide access to the meaning of a printed word. According to one route, the words are directly connected to the lexicon of meanings stored in the brain, without sounding out the words. According to the second route, orthographic information is matched with an internal visual representation of the word in the lexicon (Rayner et al. 2001). The ancient ideographic writing also represented concepts found in the lexicon without verbal intervention (The Alphabet Makers 1990, p. 17).

68. Such as those of Ratcliff (1978), Hintzman (1986), Gillund and Shiffrin (1984).

69. Gillund and Shiffrin 1984.

70. Lowe 1985. Another possibility is that exposure to a stimulus leads to an internalized trace of that stimulus. As more instances are stored, performance improves because more relevant instances can be retrieved, and the time required to retrieve them decreases. Also, objects may be recognized by comparing them to stored photograph-like images (Goldstone 1998).

71. Recognition by components theory; 36 three-dimensional geons are hypothesized (Biederman 1987).

72. These are the gestalt laws of proximity, similarity, closure, good continuation, bilateral symmetry, familiarity (Kanizsa 1979).

73. When followed by an effective mask, a letter string need only be presented for a few tens of milliseconds (msec) for it to be accurately read. (Without a mask, only about 5 msec is required.) However, the brain takes longer to interpret the string. The matching process for letter strings in skilled readers may be completed by about 140 msec after a saccade to that string. The tuned responding to the letter pattern in later visual areas (such as the fusiform gyrus in humans) starts about 90 msec after an image is painted on the retina and a distinctive neural code distinguishing that pattern from other patterns is available about 50 msec later. This estimate comes from the data for tuned responding of cells to faces in the inferior temporal region of the macaque (Irving Biederman, personal communication, February 10, 2002.)

74. Petersen et al. 1990, but later research is ambivalent.

75. Before printing became common, the probability of reading large amounts of text was limited. Yet, the perceptual complexity of all scripts suggests that those who used them throughout the centuries could quickly distinguish among similar features handwritten by different people. In organized schools of older

societies, such as madrasas or ancient Greek schools, learners were children. Perhaps learners of scripts during centuries when human lives were short tended to be children or adolescents, who acquired automaticity and slowly modified scripts as adults.

76. For features of letters critical for recognition see Gibson and Levin 1975, also Gibson et al. 1962, Gibson and Pick 2000.

77. Gradual shape changes over the centuries may make some letters too similar, and then adjustments are made to differentiate them. This process probably produced various scripts such as the Indian scripts deriving from ancient Brahmi or the development of Hebrew, Arabic, and Greek from Phoenician ideograms. (See also Sampson 1985, Harris 1990.)

78. For more detail on important concepts of perceptual learning see Goldstone 1998, Venezky 2001.

79. Karni and Sagi 1993, cited in Sekuler and Blake 2001, p. 231.

80. Schoups, Vogels and Orhan 1995, cited in Sekuler and Blake 2001, p. 231. Also Neisser 1964.

81. Review by Goldstone 1998.

82. This is called topological imprinting (Goldstone 1998).

83. See, for example, Elio and Anderson 1981. There is more transfer of learning to new items that fit a category generalization partly rather than completely. Transfer may be facilitated if the new items to be learned are in the same category but also if higher-order category information can be abstracted from a partial overlap of categories.

84. Perhaps neoliterates may not see the calligraphic and the typical fonts as having features that partly overlap and may not be able to abstract higher-order information about general features of letters written in different fonts (see, for example, Elio and Anderson 1981).

85. Rayner et al. 2001; p. 40.

86. Goldstone 1998.

87. Goteti Bala Krishnamurty, personal communication, 2000.

88. Connecting items physically improves the probability that they will be perceived together, but physically contiguous and separate displays do not show much difference in unitization (Goldstone et al. 2001).

89. Training on visual discrimination involving certain shapes improves performance on a tactile discrimination involving the same shapes (Goldstone 1998).

90. Goteti Bala Krishnamurthy, personal communication, June 2000.

91. Harris and Hatano 1999; p. 25.

92. James M. Royer, personal communication, 2002.

93. Ardila et al. 2000a.

94. For example, the 33 sounds of Italian are spelled with only 25 letters or letter combinations (Paulesu 2001). By contrast, the 40 sounds of English can be spelled with about 1,100 combinations, if unusually pronounced words are considered (Richard Venezky, personal communication, 2001).

95. Lukatela 1995.

96. Comings et al. 1992, p. 212–226; Okech et al. 1999.

97. In most respects, reading is unlike flying a plane or riding a bicycle, which once learned are not forgotten. These skills involve a continuous or closed loop skill, in which each action provides the cue for the next. In contrast, typing is an open loop skill, where each keystroke involves a separate response to a discrete stimulus (Baddeley 1999, p. 118–120).

98. Rabia 1995; Salmi 1987. Topological imprinting is required for Arabic reading. In perceptual terms, Arabic words approximate Chinese ideograms. Children may learn to assign possible pronunciations to the word configurations without breaking them down into letters, and they are more capable of perceiving units than adults.

99. Ayari 1995.

100. Wisher 1992.

101. There are some 'tricks' that may increase long-term recall, but their utility in literacy acquisition is unknown. Wilkinson et al. (2002) found that chewing gum improved working memory and subsequent recall by 35 percent in some immediate and delayed recall tasks. This may be due to increased heart rate and availability of glucose to the brain. Also, the hippocampus, which mediates short-term memory, has insulin receptors.

102. Okech et al. 1999.

103. Ahmed and Lohani 2001.

104. Roy and Kapoor 1975.

105. Comings 1995.

106. Jules Kinda on relapse into illiteracy in Burkina Faso (personal communication 2002). Observations showed that the sounds of vowels might be remembered more easily than consonants.

107. There are two traditional theories of forgetting. One argues that the memory trace simply fades and the other that forgetting occurs because memory traces are disrupted or obscured by subsequent learning (proactive and retroactive inhibition). Interference is usually a more important factor in forgetting than a faded memory trace (Baddeley 1999). A more recent theory of disuse suggests that information does not decay, but may become inaccessible due to a lack of practice (Robert Bjork, 2002, personal communication).

108. Bjork and Bjork 1992.

109. Statement of a neoliterate in rural Burkina Faso to linguistics professor Jules Kinda.

110. For example, Italian children achieve near perfect mastery of coding skills around the middle or close to the end of the first grade (Harris and Hatano 1999, p. 17). In the United States, children need longer to become expert decoders, but they do so by grade 4 (Royer 1997).

111. Chall (1983), working with children, postulated six reading stages: (0): Prereading, birth to Age 6; (1) Initial reading, or decoding stage, grades 1–2.5, ages 6–7; (2) Confirmation, fluency, ungluing from print, grades 2–3, ages 7–8; (3) Reading for learning new material, grades 4–8, ages 8–14; (4) Multiple view-

points, high school, ages 14–18; (5) Construction and reconstruction, a world view, college, age 18 and above. Others consider fewer stages, often four (Sticht 1997).

112. Attempts to teach literacy to older Portuguese illiterates also resulted in lack of fluent reading, but this may have been because of instructional deficiencies, motivational factors, or too little time spent in class (Alexandra Reis, K.M. Petersson, personal communication, October 2001).

113. Jules Kinda, personal communication, 2001.

114. Fujisawa 2001.

115. A study in the United States showed that the same orthographic and phonological processes appear to govern adults in literacy classes and schoolchildren, but correlations between word reading and spelling were weaker for adults (Greenberg et al. 1999).

116. Also observed in West Africa by Easton (1998). Graduates of Koranic schools, who read a local language in the Arabic script easily learned to read the same language with Latin characters.

117. Abadzi 1996.

118. In perceptual terms, foreigners may encounter some difficulties learning a new script because dimensions of objects that were once relevant become irrelevant (Goldstone et al. 2001). For example, a Greek pi may be formed by the Hindi letters ga or sha, and a Greek reader may see the two parallel letters as a unit in Hindi, where they are not a unit.

119. For example, younger and older adults reduce with practice the time needed to decide the number of items in a display or in memory (Fisk et al. 1988, 1990; Fisk and Rogers 1991; Madden 1983; Madden and Nebes 1980; Plude and Hoyer 1981; Plude et al. 1983; Salthouse and Somberg 1982, Salthouse 1991). However, older adults may be less capable than young adults of acquiring automaticity in visual tasks; given the same amount of practice, young adults acquire automaticity faster (Fisk et al. 1988; Fisk et al. 1990). Other studies showed small or no differences, particularly when the search is through items in memory than through a visual display.

120. The failure-to-success ratio has been reported to be 1 to 1 for trainees under the age of 35, 4.7 to 1 for trainees over the age of 35, and as high as 7.4 to 1 for trainees over the age of 39 (Cobb, Lay, and Bourdet 1971; Trites 1963; Trites and Cobb 1964a and 1964b).

121. Bortfeld and Whitehurst 2001. The authors consider that a possible developmental period for reading is cultural and exogenous rather than biological and endogenous, but they base this conclusion partly on a belief that adult literacy programs worldwide are successful (p. 177).

122. Michael Merzenich, Virginia Berninger, Richard Venezky; personal communications in 2000–2001.

123. Lennenberg 1967. The earlier maturation of children in some countries may mean that the window of opportunity to learn languages or even fluent reading might become narrower.

124. Sekuler and Blake 2001, p. 250.

125. St. Sauver et al. 2001.
126. Berkman et al. 2002.
127. Delaney-Black et al. 2002.
128. Levinger 1992.
129. The main cause of reading disabilities is phonological rather than orthographic difficulties and sometimes problems with processing language. Dyslexics have microscopic flaws in their left temporal lobes, where the language centers are located. Some have trouble with oral language, such as processing the speed, rhythm and pitch of sound and a reduced ability to distinguish between two sounds played in succession less than 1/5 of a second apart. The neural connections between the language centers and the rest of the brain are thrown into confusion. Many fMRI and PET studies show that language-processing centers in the brain do not light up for dyslexics the same way they do for others when they read. The studies have found atypical neural connections between language centers during reading and phonological processing tasks (Rumsey et al. 1997, Paulesu et al. 1996).

130. Shaywitz 1998, Shaywitz et al. 2002. Reading gains in dyslexic adults are associated with compensatory engagement of right hemisphere perisylvian areas and the left fusiform/lingual gyrus (Flowers et al. 2001). Any relevance to unschooled adults is unexplored. The reading circuits appear to be in place by about age 6 (Gaillard et al. 2003).

131. Dyslexics thus may have a problem with general sensory discrimination (Kujala et al. 2001). Some disabled readers are less able to detect visually the motion of objects (Zeffiro and Eden 2000). For some reason, the confused neural connections also affect motor skills, and dyslexics often have very bad handwriting.

132. Paulesu et al. 2001. French readers have intermediate-level difficulties.

133. Zeffiro and Eden 2000.

134. Kujala et al. 2001. After training of seven weeks, those who went through the program were able to read more words and read a bit more quickly than untrained children were. Also see Neergard 2001.

135. For example, a computerized educational game (called Fast ForWord) may retrain sound-processing brain regions. The sounds may be drawn out until a learner learns to recognize them and then gradually sped up to normal (Merzenich et al. 1996). But this method has been controversial.

136. Friedman and Alexander 1984, Henderson et al. 1985, Lott and Friedman 1999, Lott et al. 1994, 1999.

137. Perhaps middle-aged women's dropping estrogen levels (affecting the hippocampus that mediates short-term memory) also influence the ability to learn fluent reading.

138. It should be possible to present strings of words to neoliterates and ask them to rapidly identify if they are the same or different. If participants correctly identify pattern similarity but cannot read the words in the allotted time, the problem is in the decoding and interpretation rather than recognition of patterns.

# 3
# Instructional and Social Issues of Literacy Acquisition

Perceptual and cognitive factors aside, the reality of literacy classrooms, materials, methodology, and teacher preparation is what determines how much people will learn and retain. Bureaucracy, teacher absenteeism, and even the weather may shorten courses; when classes meet, time on task may be limited. Learners may find classes boring and attend infrequently. The main issues are discussed below.

## Course Duration

Generally, learners are expected to become literate and numerate with four to nine months of part-time and often necessarily irregular participation in classes. Courses usually last one or two hours per day, and they may meet daily or a few times a week. Considerable literature exists on the minimum number of instructional hours necessary to impart literacy. It is often calculated based on the rough number of days a teacher needs to present the basics of literacy and allow practice of the material. Languages written phonetically with few irregularities or complexities may require less time to teach, particularly in literate environments (where practice is readily available through store signs and newspapers). The Mexican National Adult Literacy Institute offers courses of only 40 contact hours. Similarly, Serbian women attending just one month of classes have been known to acquire basic decoding skills in the Cyrillic script.[1] On the other hand, the syllabic Indian scripts, which have many letter combinations, require longer training; in Bangladesh, where about 90 distinct letters or combinations must be taught, at least 420 hours are recommended.[2] In countries with less environmental literacy, longer courses have also been proposed, for example, 360 hours[3] or 250–300 hours in Senegal. In Cape Verde, adults are expected to progress through three phases in three years.

Ultimately, course duration is determined by administrative factors: the school-year calendar, teacher availability and appointments, textbook delivery. Delays may shorten the time. Duration and scheduling must dovetail with learners' occupations. Market days, harvests, and various activities may interrupt courses. (For example, in rural Burkina Faso courses can only take place between January and June, between harvest and the start of the rains.) Thus, the management of literacy programs involves some difficult challenges. Relatively few people are able to devote extensive time to literacy, and lengthening courses is not practical. Adults, especially married women, have a great deal of work. (Conceivably, selected illiterates could receive scholarships or financial aid to attend classes.)

Since duration does not necessarily correspond to participants' learning needs, many may acquire few skills by the end of a course. For example, NGO-led literacy classes in rural Burkina Faso last, in principle, 360 hours (4 hours a day for 90 days in the Mooré language), but at the end, participants may be hesitant readers, heavily dependent on context and guessing. Serbian women who had attended literacy classes for a month could read simple words, aided by their relatives over the years, but even the best read slowly from a second grade textbook and made many errors.[4] In these short courses, limited attention is paid to vocabulary and comprehension strategies.

To strengthen the skills of the newly literate, post-literacy courses are promoted for more extensive practice. However, the need is often longer periods of basic literacy rather than post-literacy. The problem of how to keep people in class long enough to learn basic reading under inefficient conditions has no easy solutions.

## The Challenge of Teaching Basic Numeracy

Numeracy is beyond the scope of this paper, and research regarding this topic is not presented here. It is mentioned because it is almost always taught along with literacy, but limited time may be spent on it. Acquiring automaticity in numeracy is important, not only in number identification, but in doing calculations effortlessly. If a learner must mentally count the answer to a simple problem, more complex arithmetic problems will be impossible to solve. Early step information that is essential to problem solution will have been erased from working memory before the syllogism is completed.

It is likely that many neoliterates fail to acquire automaticity in numeracy. About 32 percent of the literacy graduates tested in a large Uganda evaluation study[5] mentioned that they did not use the numeracy skills taught to them. Other studies indicate that numeracy is forgotten more easily than literacy, that women often score lower (possibly because they use numeracy less), and that certain concepts (such as decimal places) are particularly difficult for neoliterates.[6] It is also important to keep counting in one language that the learners know rather than change codes, as some countries do with primary schools. Learning multiplication and basic addition tables by heart may be important, because it may shorten the time needed for problem solving. But this is not usually done in literacy classes.

The ability to add and subtract is innate and has been identified in babies a few months old. Illiterates do have a numeracy system in their minds (however imperfect and error-prone) before they enter literacy classes. It is apparently unknown how the formal system taught in literacy classes substitutes for the one(s) illiterates already use, or how permanent the substitution is. It is possible that the old system interferes with the new, and this may be one reason why numeracy may be more easily forgotten. The systems that illiterates use to count and to calculate were researched in earlier years,[7] but findings have not been used to improve literacy programs. Perhaps literacy courses should try to improve the numeracy systems of illiterates or to link the old with the new rather than substitute for them with incompatible methods doomed to fall into disuse.

### Implications for Instruction
### Teaching Numeracy

To improve the automaticity of calculations, the building block skills might need to be automatized, such as learning multiplication tables by heart. Rather than focus on the abstract, which the unschooled may not handle well, calculations should focus on local currency and transactions, since neoliterates very much want to avoid being cheated.

## Textbook Content and Time on Task for Reading

Large-scale efforts have been made over the years to develop textbooks with topics that correspond to adults' interests and that give useful health and family planning messages. Associations focused on producing income sometimes develop their own textbooks with relevant terminology, such as practices of crops, cooperatives, savings, credit, management, and marketing.[8]

However, the textbook content may not matter as much as has been hypothesized. Learners must first and foremost spend as much time reading as possible, and if they are not automatic readers, their comprehension may be limited. Context certainly helps decode words, but practice may matter more than content relevance.[9] For example, the REFLECT methodology does not use textbooks and generates materials from the learners' own interests, but it has low success rates in reading. This may be due in part to the low exposure that learners have to texts. By contrast, the successful Total Literacy Campaign of Ajmer (India) used the textbooks of local primary schools: 85 percent of the learners passed the reading, writing, and calculating tests.[10] Nevertheless, it may be useful to structure textbooks and present letters and words according to learning research findings.

Textbooks are of little use if learners have *eyesight problems*. Nearly all adults above age 40 have some degree of presbyopia. Female Kenyan participants in an ethnological study often complained of inability to see the blackboard from a distance, of itchy eyes when they looked at white paper, and of farsightedness.[11] The poor quality of blackboards and the low light in many classrooms probably contribute to the problem. Rudimentary eye tests incorporated in the instruction of the first few days could identify such individuals early before they become discouraged by their apparent learning difficulties.

## *Use of Class Time*

Often literacy classes have a format that appears to have arisen out of common sense and years of application. A teacher reads or points to letters, and learners repeat. Subsequently, one learner may read, and the others may repeat. Little attention is given to individual learners, who may choose to repeat words or stay silent. Informal classroom observations carried out by the author found that participants are often lost and may not be reading with the class (Box 2).

## The Challenges of Teacher Selection and Training

The most important part of a literacy program is a teacher who shows up to teach. The attendance data of literacy teachers are rarely collected, but absenteeism is often mentioned as a problem. To increase accountability several literacy programs ask participants to select teachers from the community.[12] Literacy programs typically pay very low salaries, and some pay no money, remunerating teachers with food or gifts, such as sewing machines or bicycles. Teaching literacy is often seen as teaching letters, a skill that anyone with basic education can teach, and therefore not of much wage value. The low remuneration keeps program budgets low, but also keeps the teacher supply low and turnover high. Thus, a teacher corps does not get built up.

Teachers often have limited education, and may be literacy graduates themselves. Though neoliterates are often very motivated and dedicated, they may have limited understanding of how reading works and how to teach it effectively, having as role models their own literacy and primary school teachers. For example, in Burkina Faso, one teacher was observed telling learners to read more slowly rather than faster. They would be hard pressed to teach the more cognitively sophisticated and effective strategies presented in this document.

Teacher training frequently lasts five days or less and may focus on how to proceed with the literacy textbook and take attendance. Often it includes exhortations to treat learners with respect and to be a facilitator rather than a teacher. Teachers may be told that adults do not learn like children. This advice is certainly needed, but training courses may not instill effective teaching techniques. Little remediation is possible later, because supervision tends to be spotty. Teachers may need longer training and supervision to form learners' groups and supervise them in order to increase time on task. However, the turnover and limited selection caused by the extremely low remuneration in many countries create obstacles.

---

### Box 2. Literacy Learners May Get Limited Practice

It is afternoon in an adult literacy class run by an NGO in a rural school in the Mooré-speaking area of Burkina Faso in October 2000. The village women, all completely unschooled, have finished most of their agricultural work of the season, and about 40 of them are in class, along with several small children and a few men. The teacher asks people to read. One person reads 3–4 words and the class repeats. Some learners are following the text in the book. Others repeat, but point to the wrong place in the page. Still others repeat while looking away from the books.

In July 2001, a similar scene takes place in a well-monitored women's class run by an NGO in a Wolof-speaking town of Senegal. All but two of the 23 women went to school as children. On the board there is a story about their daily lives, and women take turns reading the text. The text is short, and after a few repetitions, the next reader recites it by heart. While one learner reads, the rest are inactive, fiddling with the items on their desks or looking out the window. All women can identify the words on the blackboard, except for the two who started the class as complete illiterates; they are barely able to put letters together. The teacher was not aware of the difficulties these two women had.

---

*Source:* Author's data.

The outcome is that literacy teachers may teach learners for limited periods of time and use inadequate methodology. The modest project outcomes coupled with the number of teachers needed create a vicious circle, with governments and donors unwilling to pay for programs that include substantial waste.

Given the low pay and lack of a real career, the individuals likely to become teachers may also have little time to devote to teacher training and little motivation to do better. In some very poor areas, however (such as rural Burkina Faso), they may be respected as promoters and may be more willing to devote the time to serve their constituents. Community participation in the choice of teachers often brings forth more accountable individuals.

### Implications for Instruction
### Classroom Time and Teacher Training

Situations where one learner is engaged while the rest wait for their turn or just repeat what is said waste class time. Time can be better used if students read to each other in small groups (reciprocal teaching). However, they must be monitored for mistakes, and the teacher must be trained in organizing and monitoring group work.

Teacher training must improve substantially, in terms of content as well as social issues. Training should include the basics of the cognitive principles needed to develop automaticity, phonological awareness, and working memory. However, the low education of teachers must be taken into account. One viable training means is to use videotaped role modeling, which would show examples of effective and ineffective instruction. Countries that support high-technology media, such as India and South Africa, may use computer-based instruction.[13]

Teachers could ask learners whether they can see certain designs on their books or on the blackboard and seat those who cannot see well nearer the blackboard. It is possible that some of the dropout and low skills are due to this problem.

## Group Formation and Livelihood Training

Evaluations of programs in Guinea, Kenya, Senegal, and Uganda suggest that illiterates may prefer courses that include learning how to earn a living and get access to credit.[14] For example, courses in Kenya which offer such opportunities were found to have 80 percent attendance rates, while literacy-only courses had 20 percent attendance. Income-oriented training sometimes becomes a "literacy second" approach; groups implement schemes to generate income, and at some point they realize that they need literacy. Then they become interested learners. Some other programs teach literacy and income generation at the same time or demand completion of a basic literacy course before allowing entrance to income generation.

The preference for livelihood training may not be well founded. Though some participants may have slightly increased incomes, outcomes are generally disappointing.[15] This may be due to the rudimentary knowledge imparted and lack of support through business development and management. Literacy instructors often do not know enough to teach livelihood training or income-generation activities, and separate cadres of instructors create logistical difficulties and expenses.

*Group formation to achieve a goal* for which literacy is merely a means has been more successful. Participants stay motivated and focused on the goal. For example, a group of women in rural Burkina Faso learned to read and write in order to keep accounts of transactions at the village mill (Association Manegdbzanga). An observational study was carried out in 40 communities with group formation of five West African countries (Burkina Faso, Ghana, Mali, Niger, and Senegal). The study did not evaluate how expertly learners could read or how sustainable their skills were. However, it concluded that the large majority of adults under 50 (and many older) can learn to read, write, and handle practical arithmetic in their mother tongue or another well-known language without difficulty if provided with solid motivation, a reasonably sound instructional method, participatory activities, and real opportunities for application.[16]

There are sound reasons why reading groups may promote better reading skills. Group pressure may encourage participants to stay on and persevere, while clearly knowing the benefits of certain information items has been shown to make them more memorable.[17] With a constant business need to read, extra practice is continuous, and one's livelihood depends on deciphering the material. Also, the people who form groups and stay in them are highly selected, and may have above-average ability levels.

### Implications for Instructional Group Formation

Group formation or livelihood training are effective under rather limited circumstances. How-ever, its appeal can be expanded. The rudiments of money management and numeracy can be introduced early on in general literacy courses so as to attract and keep many of the participants interested in income generation.

## Social Benefits of Adult Literacy Programs

*"I feel enlightened.... When something is written on the blackboard, I am able to copy."*[18]

Overall, participation in literacy has a strong social dimension. Most evaluations and reviews referenced in this document mention the self-confidence, empowerment, and attitude changes that participants receive from literacy classes.[19] For example, Kenyan female learners in an ethnographic study talked about the desire to live well, to open eyes, to be enlightened. The individual empowerment effects are reportedly strong and well documented, and adult basic education is considered a means by which women can take charge of their lives.[20] Some literacy graduates in Ghana had reportedly become more articulate than those who did not join the program.[21] REFLECT evaluations and documents extensively discuss the empowerment benefits of the program.[22]

World Bank sector documents[23] point to various studies that have defined the impact of literacy projects as confidence, autonomy, empowerment, more effective oral (and sometimes written) communication, decontextualized language use, improved family health, more productive livelihoods, and support of children's education. The effects of primary-school education on learners' quality of life, health, fertility, and productivity are well known. However, it is unclear how literacy program participants obtain those benefits. Some health and social messages are transmitted during classes, but the studies do not state whether the social benefits to participants are a result of these messages or of information acquired through independent reading.

Since the reading level acquired in literacy classes is often modest, the purported effects are puzzling. They imply that learners may get the empowerment and other social benefits without necessarily becoming literate. If so, this is encouraging. For example, Nepalese women who had attended longer courses reported more empowerment than participants in shorter courses or non-participants.[24] But what instructional features produce self-confidence across the many countries where they are reported? If learners do not get the skill that enables them to gain confidence in reading, what are they self-confident about? How long does the effect last with non-literates? And do learners stay self-confident if they lapse back into illiteracy?

## Box 3. REFLECT: Beneficiaries May Feel Empowered but Not Be Literate

The Regenerated Freirean Literacy through Empowerment Community Techniques (REFLECT) helps groups identify local issues and problems of shared concern through visual materials that are generated in each community: maps, matrices, calendars, or diagrams. Participants are encouraged to communicate about and act upon the problems. Also, they learn to recognize the words of the problems they identify through a whole-word method. Reportedly the approach interweaves literacy with empowerment and creates motivation, confidence, and self-esteem, particularly for women.[25] Participants do not typically use textbooks; they generate their own according to their particular needs. Also, their literacy performance is not tested; at the end of the course, they are asked to estimate their reading ability on a rating scale.

REFLECT has spread rapidly from small-scale programs in 25 countries to more than 350 organizations in 60 countries that include governments and NGOs. There are training and coordination units in countries such as Bangladesh, Brazil, El Salvador, Ghana, India, Mali, Mozambique, Nepal, Pakistan, Peru, South Africa, and Uganda; 250,000 participants were in the program in August 2000.

In its earlier stages, the project had high rates of participant retention (69 percent) and reported rates of achieved literacy of over 60 percent (Salvador, 86 percent; Bangladesh, 77.5 percent; Uganda, 99 percent).[26] However, subsequent evaluations report mixed results.[27] In Bangladesh, 50 percent of the participants enrolled in the course "circles" could read a paragraph and make basic calculations up to 100 after attending for a year. But for three sites of India, at least 50 percent of the participating women were unable or unwilling to learn literacy. Evaluators estimated that only about 25 percent of the Indian participants were becoming literate. Those who did were generally the younger persons in the circles. The others could identify and write words that had arisen in the course of the construction of the graphics, but they were unable to decipher most of the letters. People often dropped out when the program started teaching individual letters.[28]

Although this program was initially billed as a means to teach literacy, this activity is now just one option. Participants decide what to work on, and less than a quarter of them take up reading.[29] Perhaps the method confers significant empowerment and development benefits to its participants, as self-reports indicate. However, without control groups, baseline data, random assignments, and measurements on important variables, it is impossible to know.

*Source:* Abadzi 2003a.

No answers have been found in the literature. Also, no analyses have been found that related reading achievement with self-confidence. The evaluation study of a Ugandan program[30] assessed attitude changes in conjunction with reading and found that "modern" attitudes and ideas were related to higher reading scores. However, this was not interpreted as a necessary effect of literacy classes, because many nonliterates also gave "modern" answers to questions. There were no baseline data to compare beliefs or empowerment level before the classes. It is therefore conceivable that those who were already more self-confident or "modern" thinkers attended the classes. Furthermore, belief statements are not tantamount to behavioral changes.[31]

The measurement of self-confidence and empowerment is typically based on self-reports, that may be impressionistic,[32] post hoc, often with no baseline measures. Memory bias is a widespread phenomenon, and people may report opinions to show themselves in a favorable light. For example, an ethnographic researcher[33] asked Kenyan female participants questions such as: "Do you think you have achieved something since you joined the class? If yes, please describe." "Do you think you have changed since you joined the classes? If yes, how do you feel about the changes?" Teachers were asked: "Do you think your learners have changed since they joined the class? If yes, what kinds of changes have you observed?" Participants attributed considerable benefits to their class, including better marital relations and knowledge how to behave, boiling water to clean latrines, income generation, enlightenment from copying letters, and higher self-esteem by becoming more knowledgeable. However, the literacy teacher was a woman of low education who lived among the participants; it was unclear how the learners obtained this knowledge from her and whether they modified their behavior accordingly. The teacher attributed significant benefits to the literacy classes; for example, she said that women dressed better than they used to and that the relationships among them had improved. Nevertheless, the number of literacy sessions was limited; during the rainy season, the class was frequently canceled because both the learners and the teacher were busy with agricultural work. The study did not include baseline answers to these questions or observations to verify the extent to which these benefits were taught or how they took place.

One possible explanation may be *researcher bias and social desirability of responses*. The one Nepalese study that reported empowerment as a function of length of literacy course duration[34] leaves open the possibility that women learned during class the answers expected from them and that non-participants did not know the desirable answers. Another possible explanation is *cognitive illusions*. For example, illusions of competence are well documented in the psychological literature.[35] After powerful learning experiences, people may gain a sense of understanding without having achieved the level of knowledge required to perform adequately in the real world. Therefore, they believe they know more than they do. For example, a learner reported during an ethnographic research[36] that she could read "a little" but then demonstrated that she was unable to read letters she was receiving.

Empowerment may also happen because of *group dynamics* and camaraderie, or because participants may feel that class attendance gives them improved social status. Group dynamics can produce desirable changes toward poverty alleviation. But if empowerment is acquired merely through group membership or feeling that one belongs among the schooled, then it is a "placebo" effect, whose development value may be dubious.

Many reports discuss empowerment benefits,[37] so it is possible that they exist independently of measurement artifacts or memory tricks. It is difficult at this stage to establish a cause-effect link between literacy courses and social benefits, including self-confidence and empowerment. Clearly, more behaviorally oriented research is needed to sift through the possible explanations and verify the extent and sustainability of social benefits to literacy instruction.

### *Implications for Instruction*
### Measuring Social Benefits

Program organizers must be quite clear about what empowerment benefits they should reasonably expect and how to bring them about. If a program has empowerment objectives, they should be worked into the curriculum timeframe, and teachers should be explicitly instructed on activities to be undertaken. To minimize memory bias of researchers and participants, baseline responses should be obtained to show change, including control groups if possible.

# Notes

1. Ardila et al. 2000a; Lukatela et al. 1995.
2. Task force conclusions in Abadzi 1994, p. 11.
3. Diagne 1999, p. 19; Oxenham et al. 2002.
4. Lukatela et al. 1995.
5. Okech et al. 1999, 2001.
6. Jennings 1990; New Era 1989, 1990.
7. For example, Gay and Cole 1967; Cole and Means 1981.

8. For example, ACOPAM, cited in Oxenham et al. 2002 p.29.
9. African Muslim children often learn to read the Koran and many become automatic readers without any knowldge of Arabic.
10. External evaluation team 1993; mentioned in Oxenham and Aoki 2002.
11. Fujisawa 2001. About 51 percent of all people in the United States have refraction problems (American Optometric Association 1992).
12. Diagne 1999, p. 12, 44.
13. The International Literacy Institute has produced a multimedia teacher training CD ROM called the International Literacy Explorer, that is also Internet based.
14. Oxenham et al. 2001. The preferred activity is livelihood training, because income generation projects have been shown to produce only occasional or limited income.
15. Oxenham et al. 2001.
16. Easton 1998, p. 83.
17. For example,, Perfetto et al. 1983.
18. Fujisawa 2001. Statement of a 33-year-old female Kenyan learner, who had never been to school.
19. Moulton 1997, 2001.
20. Lind 1990, 1997.
21. Korboe 1997.
22. Archer 1995, 1996; Riddell 2001.
23. "Engaging with Adults" (Lauglo 2001) and "Including the 900+ Million" (Oxenham and Aoki 2002, draft).
24. Burchfield 1997.
25. Archer and Cottingham 1995.
26. Archer and Cottingham 1995.
27. Saldanha 2000; Riddell 2001.
28. Riddell 2001.
29. ActionAid International 2001.
30. Okech et al. 1999.
31. Carr-Hill et al. 1991.
32. Riddell 2001, p. 7.
33. Fujisawa 2001.
34. Burchfield 1997.
35. Bjork 1994, 1999; Jacoby et al., 1994. Sometimes, a dynamic teacher, may make learners feel that they understand during class, but later they cannot make sense of the material.
36. Fujisawa 2001.
37. Discussions on the meaning of empowerment: e.g., Hashemi, Shuler, and Riley 1996; Jejeebhoy 1996.

# 4
# Policy Implications of Cognitive Literacy Methods

What policy actions are needed to ascertain that students in classes acquire fast and effortless reading? Governments and donors have strongly emphasized the management, planning, and institutional issues necessary for large-scale literacy programs to succeed. Better management is necessary but insufficient for improved literacy dissemination. More attention must be given to instruction. But for large-scale implementation, a clear rationale is needed for making choices.

This is where cognitive research can contribute. In contrast to educational theories that emphasize individual differences and make standardized procedures harder to establish, cognitive psychology offers broad guidelines about how people learn and forget. Though the field is still evolving, some principles can be enunciated succinctly and be operationalized.

However, relatively few people worldwide understand and can disseminate cognitive principles and their applications. Adult education specialists usually lack training in cognition and neuropsychology. Furthermore, automatic readers lack an intuitive understanding of the working-memory limitations or perceptual learning intricacies and may underestimate the complexity of literacy acquisition. Thus, the research agendas of university adult education departments and agencies worldwide focus more on social, motivational, and methodological issues. Cognitive research is rarely called upon to improve adult literacy.

Also, there are logistical obstacles in the use of more sophisticated methods that facilitate fluency and automaticity. As demonstrated in Annex A, these methods require better trained teachers, more classroom organization, and more individual performance monitoring. These prerequisites may be feasible in resource-rich environments (such as Brazil) but may be unsustainable in poorer environments, where the teachers themselves may be neoliterates. Computers are found near poor areas in only a few countries, such as in India, Brazil, and South Africa. However, dissemination of basic cognitive research findings may help. If higher-level staff of literacy agencies learn more about the implications of cognitive variables, applications may become more valued and ultimately more sustainable.

The more complex methods and longer teacher training may require higher budgetary outlays than more traditional methods. Costs per learner may increase, but costs per graduate with stable literacy skills may decrease as programs become more efficient. Governments must determine whether the increased costs of more scientifically based literacy instruction are worth the benefits and whether an increased share of education budgets for literacy instruction is justified. Clearly, trials are needed. Given the urgency to achieve Education for All by the year 2015 it may be deemed desirable to invest in and investigate this new literacy paradigm.

### *Implications for Instruction*
### Integrating Research Findings Early in Reading Classes

Perhaps all courses in all countries could devote much time in the first two weeks to the following tasks:

- Phonological awareness exercises for about 20 minutes daily.
- Learning to count through local money and transactions, discussing how to avoid being cheated.
- Digit span and other exercises (integrated within counting and phonological awareness) to help lengthen the working memory; understanding pictures in the textbook, using data in syllogisms.
- Simple visual tests to determine which learners might need to sit nearer the blackboard. (These could be included in one page of a textbook.)

Focusing on utility, for example, asking learners to bring in materials they would like to read.

## Researching Literacy Acquisition to Improve Effectiveness

Clearly, applied research is needed to determine which methods are more effective and how the costs and benefits compare. Some are of higher priority than others. Should the donor community decide to invest more in research, here is a potential agenda.

To investigate the problems of neoliterates, academic expertise is needed in perception, cognition, and neuropsychology. NGOs that teach literacy usually do not have this expertise. Grants could be given to universities in developing countries for literacy research. Because these rather specialized domains of knowledge are rare in the developing world, research must be carried out through twinning arrangements with expert academics of industrialized countries.

The various scripts and the languages that use them have specific decoding and perceptual issues. Literacy "laboratories" in ongoing classes could be set up in four or five countries that deal with specific language and script combinations: India for the use of syllabic scripts, an African country using the Latin script, a country for the Arabic language, and a country using the Arabic script in Indo-European languages (such as Afghanistan, Iran, and Pakistan). Countries that are developing institutional strength and expertise, such as Burkina Faso, could be preferred. Researchers should have access to computerized equipment for measuring various aspects of reading performance and cognition of illiterates, such as tachistometers for the study of eye saccades, and brain scanning equipment to explore brain changes as learning occurs (for example, an fMRI at the All India Medical Sciences Center in Delhi). Research would be carried out in literacy classes run by governments or NGOs, but for certain pilots, learners might be paid small sums to participate. Issues to study could include:

- The minimum level of speed and accuracy that is functional and sustainable; how people with marginal skills use written materials, and how they may compensate for low speed (for example, by reading aloud).
- Amount of reading exposure needed to automatize various letter patterns that occur in specific scripts, which patterns learners find particularly easy or difficult. What conditions facilitate progress from a serial to a parallel processing mode? Under what conditions are sounds permanently connected to letter patterns and unlikely to be forgotten?
- Comparison of adult performance with that of child learners, given similar circumstances and amount of exposure; identification of aspects in which adults and children differ in perceptual learning and acquisition of automaticity; application of the findings to improve programs for both age ranges.
- Effective audiovisual and cognitive methods to train teachers for innovative literacy instruction.
- Relapse into illiteracy: relationship with instructional duration, effectiveness, and prior schooling; characteristics of those most likely to relapse, exactly what reading features are forgotten, techniques to minimize it (for example, the utility of mnemonics) or access the lost memories.
- Study of how the brains of adult illiterates respond to training. What brain scan activation patterns change following various interventions, and how do these compare with those of expert readers and dyslexics?

- Powerful simulation models have been developed to determine the likely reading outcomes of readers who have various limitations and follow various strategies.[1] Such models could be carried out with data collected from literacy course participants to predict likely achievement levels and suggest changes in instructional strategy.

Research focused on poverty alleviation might include questions such as:

- How do illiterates use data and development messages, such as IEC (information, education, communication)? How do literacy participation and amount of formal schooling change data use? To what extent is the ability to understand media (radio, TV) messages affected by literacy level?
- What forms of interventions can improve the areas of lower cognitive performance of adult illiterates and relate learning to cognitive measures such as processing speed, inhibitory functioning, and working memory capacity? The efficacy of simple remedies such as the effects of chewing gum on the working memory could be explored for utility.
- Does an improvement in the cognitive processes of neoliterates lead to more effective decisionmaking regarding life choices that lead to poverty alleviation?
- How does empowerment relate to the degree of literacy learners acquire? What conditions maximize the empowerment attributable to literacy classes?

A research program of 3–5 years would provide considerable understanding on these issues.

## Notes

1. Rayner et al. 2001.

# Annex A
# Improving Reading Performance in Adult Literacy Classes of Burkina Faso

An opportunity to understand better the reading processes of neoliterates and apply cognitively-based insructional methods arose when the Swiss Development Cooperation agreed to finance, through its World Bank Trust Fund, evaluative research of Swiss-supported programs in Burkina Faso. This country, which has a literacy rate of only about 20 percent,[1] was chosen because it has established a tradition of income-generating group formation. Literacy is taught by the governmental National Literacy Institute (INA) as well as by many nongovernmental organizations (NGOs). Notable among them is the Swiss-financed Organisation Suisse d' Entraide Ouvrière (OSEO), which pledged its help in carrying out the research. Because of weather patterns and agricultural work, literacy classes in rural areas are carried out only from January to June of every year.

The research took place from May 2000 to August 2001 and involved: (a) baseline measurements and comparisons with U.S. norms, (b) designing interventions and assessment procedures, (c) implementing interventions, and (d) evaluating the outcomes. A follow-up phase, assessment of forgetting and relapse into illiteracy was to be carried out in the spring of 2002, but time permitted only informal observations.

A research team was assembled, consisting of Dr. James M. Royer, educational psychologist at the University of Massachusetts, Amherst, and Burkinabé researcher Dr. Jules Kinda, professor of linguistics at University of Ouagadougou, along with three Burkinabé assistants. The Burkinabé research team was given background training on the literacy issues to be investigated and was trained in the use and administration of materials as well as on practical test development and data analysis.

## Research Participants

The participants in the research were learners and graduates of literacy classes in Manegdbzanga, a rural area located about 45 kilometers outside Ouagadougou. Area residents have become known for their dedication to group formation and adult literacy activities[2] where groups learned to read in the 1980s and 1990s in order to increase their agricultural and trading productivity. Representatives of the donor community frequently visit the villagers' association of Nomgana. In this area of limited formal education, literacy classes are well attended. In addition to adult literacy and income generation, OSEO has supported a successful Mooré-French program in the local schools since about 1990. (The schools of Burkina Faso teach exclusively in French.) These children learned first to read in Mooré. Several cohorts of them have completed primary school and gone on to French-speaking secondary schools. For literacy instruction and testing, it was decided to use the Mooré language, which is spoken in Ouagadougou and its environs, including Manegdbzanga. The participants ranged in age from 7 to people in their 40s who did not know their exact age.

The researchers initially tested various groups of participants to establish baseline data. Then the reading methods were applied to 15 classes of about 250 learners, whose average age was 20. Seventy-eight percent of them had not been to school at all.

## Development and Pilot-Testing of Materials

### Computer-Assisted Measurements

Central to the measurement of reading performance was the Computer-based Academic Assessment System (CAAS). This system records the speed and accuracy of readers in letters, syllables, words, or sentences, and was originally developed for dyslexic children. A stimulus appears on the screen (such as a letter, word, or number) and the examinee responds into a microphone. The vocal response stops a clock in the computer and the examiner scores the data for accuracy. The speed and accuracy data, along with learner names and characteristics, are stored in a file on the computer and are later retrieved for statistical analysis. Measurements on speed and accuracy can be reported separately, or combined into an index.

Three notebook computers with extra batteries were purchased and carried to Ouagadougou for this purpose. Stimuli for the CAAS were prepared in Mooré by the team of linguists. Tests were developed for letters, syllables, common words, simple sentences, numerals, simple additions, and simple subtractions. Each test consisted of 20 stimuli, and their development presented some challenges. Mooré is a tonal language, which uses accents on many vowels as well as some letters taken from Greek; developing fonts for the computer displays required some work, as did the development of criteria regarding which responses would be considered acceptable, given the tonality of the language.

## *Paper and Pencil Achievement Tests*

Paper and pencil tests that measured letter identification, syllable identification, word identification, and understanding of sentences were developed in Mooré. These were multiple-choice tests, where the learners were asked to circle the correct word. Similarly, a multiple-choice test was developed for phonological awareness tasks. These were to be used as backup tests in case the electronics of CAAS failed and to double-check the CAAS results. The learners were not tested on reading aloud and listening comprehension because of the complexities involved in testing for readability of texts.

## *Questionnaire*

A questionnaire was developed in Mooré and was administered to participants orally to obtain data on demographic characteristics, including attendance in formal or Koranic school, frequency of reading use, and reasons for taking the literacy course. (See details in Appendix.)

## Baseline Measurements and Comparisons

In this phase, the research team wanted to find out how well various groups of people read in the area and to establish baselines. Comparisons were made with U.S. students, for whom data were available. Thus it would be possible to make comparisons between a literate country and a sample of Burkinabé school children and adult graduates of literacy courses. Also, the research team would thus evaluate the extent to which literacy class graduates were proficient in performing low-level reading skills. Another group of interest consisted of Burkinabé neoliterates who had become literacy teachers.

In May 2000, the researchers tested groups of residents with the CAAS and obtained speed and accuracy data for basic reading and math tasks. Results were compared with children who were (a) students in grades 1–3 of the bilingual schools; (b) adolescents attending nonformal schools for adolescents, largely financed by UNICEF; (c) secondary school students, who had completed the bilingual education primary school program; (e) graduates of literacy classes; (f) graduates of literacy classes who had become literacy teachers; (g) literacy teachers with formal education; and (h) secondary school students. The results were compared with norms of U.S. students.

The comparisons indicated that the Burkinabé adults completing one phase of adult literacy training were generally performing at a level lower than that attained by second-grade students in both Burkina Faso and the United States. More specifically:

- Students at all levels tested (rural bilingual grades 2, 3, 8, adolescent and adult nonformal classes) read more slowly and less accurately than a sample of second grade students in the United States.
- Learners in the process of completing two years of nonformal adolescent and adult classes read too slowly (about 2.2 seconds per word) and inefficiently (80–87 percent correct); given the limitations of human memory, they were probably not able to use reading extensively.
- Graduates of past years who became literacy teachers have become more efficient readers with time and approximated the speed and accuracy of formally educated literacy teachers and of secondary rural school students. Some of the tested literacy teachers, however, had scores only slightly above those of their learners.
- Student scores in basic arithmetic additions and subtractions approximated U.S. scores of the appropriate grades.

These results supported the hypothesis that adult literacy training programs may not be developing adequate low-level reading skills. Suitable methods were sought to find out if it was possible to increase the speed and accuracy of the next cohorts of literacy learners.

## Developing and Pilot-Testing Literacy Interventions

From October 2000 to February 2001, the Burkinabé research team operated a "literacy laboratory" at the Center for the Handicapped and Orphans of Sector 28 in Ouagadougou. They invited illiterate or semi-literate area residents to come for afternoon classes, in which various methods were tried and developed. About 30 people attended on a regular basis. The researchers pilot-tested various methods, observed and videotaped results, and asked the participants for their opinions regarding effectiveness. The following methods were tried:

ANNEX 81

- *Phonological awareness exercises.* These teach illiterates the structure of the language and are related to reading effectiveness. Participants learned to find the initial and final letters of words, make rhymes, and determine the number of syllables in words.
- *Speeded reading tasks of progressive difficulty.* This task was to help learners read automatically as many common words as possible, so that their working memory would not be overloaded with letter-by-letter reading. Learners received packs of 20 cards, each with one word, which they were asked to shuffle and read to each other as fast as possible. The task involved two people; one was reading, and the other was timing the reader with an inexpensive plastic stopwatch. The learners were taught to read the results and place them every day on a graph paper. Every day, the readers read the pack a little faster. After the improvement had leveled off, they were given packs with longer words. Learners went through a total of four packs that had words of three, four, or more letters.
- *Grouping of similar letters and systematic pairing of consonant and vowel combinations.* This technique was developed by the biostatistician Goteti Bala Krishamurthy, who had applied it extensively in south India. Learners were asked which consonants looked similar to them, and they learned these in groups of 4–5, in hopes of learning to discriminate among them. To help learners deduce the reading strategy by themselves, each of the consonants was paired systematically with all vowels. After learning a group of new letters, the learners were told to search for them in a local newspaper.

The learners, many of whom had briefly attended school or other literacy classes, found the activities attractive. Variability and work in small groups helped learners focus on the material much of the time. It was gratifying to see (and capture on video) the reactions of learners who, through phonological exercises, understood the structure of language. Speeded tasks created competitions, with learners reading as fast as possible while others measured them with a stopwatch. More potential learners dropped by the center every day. Sometimes they were so excited they did not want to leave at the end of the class.

However, problems were also noted. Many learners made errors when reading to each other, and these could go uncorrected when a monitor was not available nearby. Though chronometers incited learners' interest, registration of reaction times on graph paper was often incorrect. Some people, particularly women, could not read them well. Reading from cards was in some respects hard and time-consuming, since each pack had to be kept separate and not mixed up with others. Reading from sheets of paper was simpler, but then the order of the words stayed the same, and readers could memorize it. Phrases that required filling in the blanks were tried, but learners could not perform effectively, possibly because their working memory was too short to keep all the material. It was found that reading individual letters was not useful, and the lowest units presented to learners were syllables. Though writing seemed necessary, it was not emphasized in this research study.

After four months of working with the learners, the team developed appropriate tasks for phonological awareness in Mooré and feasible tasks for timing and graphing progress of progressively harder speeded reading tasks. The Krishnamurty technique for Indian languages did not perform as expected with the Roman alphabet; learners were confused rather than helped by learning the b, d, p, and q together, and the researchers realized that they did not understand what degree of similarity helps and what degree impedes learning. So, this method was set aside.

In addition to these activities, the CAAS and questionnaire were administered to instructors and neoliterates of centers in Ouagadougou. The tests were used for practice, and data were analyzed for possible significant insights to the automaticity process. However, the performance levels of the participants were nearly 100 percent in accuracy, and they did not provide important information.

## Designing the Intervention and Training Teachers

To test the efficacy of the phonological awareness tasks and speeded reading, a quasi-experimental design was developed. It involved four interventions: (a) phonological awareness training, (b) rapid reading training, (c) both phonological awareness and rapid reading, and (d) a control group involving only traditional teaching techniques, that is, one person reading and the group repeating what was read. These were carried out in literacy centers in (a) Manegdbzanga, where OSEO finances implementation during the dry season every year (January to June) and (b) Windyam, also outside Ouagadougou, where the governmental National Literacy Institute is active. Although the assignment of learners in classes was not random (due to geographic considerations), the 15 centers were randomly assigned to one of the four interventions. With nine centers sponsored by the government and nine by OSEO, 18 treatment combinations were created. It was anticipated that each of the classrooms would enroll approximately 25 learners, making a total of 250 learners participating in the study.

The original design was to have every participant complete a questionnaire and the paper-and-pencil tests at the end of the study. Because

CAAS is time-consuming and it was not possible to charge multiple batteries in rural areas without electricity, only a sample of learners could be tested with it. Thus, the plan was to randomly select five learners from each school to complete the CAAS tasks both prior to beginning instruction and upon completion of the first phase of schooling. This plan would result in CAAS assessments for 90 learners.

## Teacher Training

The first challenge was to train 24 teachers in carrying out the methods. Training was done over four days (January 8–12, 2001) at the Manegdbzanga center of Nomgana. The teachers were paid an honorarium for their attendance as well as a small stipend for implementing the experimental methods. The rationale for all methods was explained, and videotapes were shown, which had been recorded during the operation of the "literacy laboratory." Then the teachers, many of them themselves graduates of literacy classes, were asked to perform the tasks. They found the training very interesting but also very brief. A refresher training would have been useful, but for logistical reasons, it was never carried out. It would have been helpful to measure teacher performance and use it as an explanatory variable in the treatment and control groups, but time did not permit this procedure.

A random sample of learners was pretested through the CAAS. It was determined that most could not read at all, although a few recognized a few letters. Eighty-one percent of them had not been to school at all, while most of the remaining 18 percent reported attending for one year. Thus, no pretest paper-and-pencil test was applied. Also, the assumption was made that experimental and control groups were similar at the beginning of treatment, allowing a comparison of the post-test results only. The number of years of school correlated only .09 with final reading scores. Because Burkina Faso has a literacy rate of only about 20 percent, it was unlikely that participants learned reading outside formal or nonformal classrooms.

## Implementing Instruction

### Learners

The subjects for the experimental part of the study were 425 participants of literacy classes. There were more females (295) than males (131) enrolled. The mean reported age of the learners was 20. Forty-two percent of the learners were married and 32 percent were single. One hundred thirty five of the learners reported they had at least one child. The number of children the learners reported having ranged from 1 to 9. About 78 percent had never been to school, and about 22 percent of the learners had some previous formal schooling. The shortest time attendance period was 1 year, and the longest was 3 years. Twenty-eight learners reported having gone to a Koranic school, and may have known some Arabic reading. Their competency in Arabic was not tested.

Since literacy is a desirable activity in Burkina Faso and a form of social gathering for rural residents, more people attended than was expected. The subjects who found out about the classes and decided to come and thus were self-selected. (No surveys were done to determine which residents had decided not to come and for which reasons, therefore, the criteria for self-selection are unknown.) All were from farming families, although their specific socioeconomic status was not known. Parental formal education was not known, but was probably non-existent.

## Classroom Observations

The classes were observed at least once a week by the research team. The teachers largely implemented the methods as expected and were given help when they did not. The researchers only corrected issues related to the implementation of the methods; they did not offer suggestions for the instructional improvement of the literacy class curricula, although several examples were presented. For example, one teacher initially instructed learners to read slowly, although the goal of literacy classes should be rapid, effortless reading.

The research team provided materials for the classes to carry out the two treatments: (a) word lists for phonological awareness and sheets for learners to register what differences they heard in words; (b) stopwatches, graph sheets, packs of cards with words of varying difficulties as well as sheets with lists of words. These were printed and local print shops. Stopwatches (one for every two learners) were bought for 2000 CFAF ($2.50) each at the local market.

Classes met for two hours daily, and learners practiced the experimental methods for about 30 minutes in class each day. For the remaining time, learners practiced decoding skills and took turns reading aloud while other learners repeated. This methodology does not use class time well, but it is widely used, and the researchers did not intervene to change it.

Again, the researchers observed that the activity level required by progressive speeded tasks was a welcome departure from the usual read-and-repeat method. Generally, learners became able to time their classmates, read stopwatches, and record time on simple graphs. The phonological awareness tasks also worked well, but they were time-consuming as presented, and the method needed more refinement.

# Annex

Because the methods were applied in different villages that had some distance among them, it is highly unlikely that there were contamination effects from one classroom to another.

## *Evaluating the Impact of the Instructional Interventions—Data Challenges*

Because of delays and administrative difficulties, only 15 centers could be used in the study, but the number of participants was much larger than the 250 planned. Reading tests and a questionnaire were administered to a total of 425 learners. Of these, 198 were enrolled in classrooms conducted by OSEO staff and 227 were enrolled in classrooms conducted by INA staff.

Field research in relatively remote rural areas inevitably runs into the unexpected. OSEO classes were underway in early February, but government-financed (INA) classes did not start until the end of March. The INA learners received only three months of instruction by the time the rains arrived in June, while the OSEO learners had five months of instruction.

Five learners from each class were to be chosen and tested at random using CAAS. Although three batteries were provided for each notebook, frequent electrical blackouts and perhaps the 45 degrees centigrade heat in the villages (where there was no electricity) contributed to the deterioration of the batteries. Each would last 20 minutes or so, and they often ran out in the middle of a test, losing the results. Thus, researchers could not test the number of learners expected. Overall, only 37 learners could be assessed through the CAAS in pre- and post-tests, and these were not distributed evenly in the various classes. Therefore, the analyses of these data were not included in this report.

Near the end of the course, learners answered a questionnaire that collected demographic information, and they completed tests (in their native language) that measured their competence at identifying letters, syllables, words, and sentence length material. Obtaining demographic data from learners also posed some problems. About 30 learners stated that they had never before attended literacy class or school, but displayed rudimentary reading skills during the pretest. Apparently literacy classes are a social function in the villages, and residents did not want to be excluded.

Because the experimental conditions were imperfect, the data were "noisy" with more error variance than expected. Efforts were made to understand the effects of the treatments and disentangle them from related variables. The observational data collected (including videotaped sessions) provided qualitative information to supplement the statistical analyses.

## Results of the Intervention Efforts

Analyses of variance were carried out, comparing the various treatment groups in OSEO, INA, and control classes. Performance on the tests administered near the end of phase one training indicated that learners enrolled in courses sponsored by OSEO performed better than did learners enrolled in government-sponsored courses. Given that the government courses had lasted a shorter period, this result was not surprising.

The results on the paper-and-pencil tests also showed that the learners receiving any of the new instructional interventions tended to perform better on the tests than did the learners enrolled in the control schools. There were 20 possible comparisons between treatment and control schools; the treatment groups scored higher than the control group in 18 of the 20. Moreover, in 13 of these 18 comparisons the advantage for the treatment group over the control group was statistically significant. In the two comparisons favoring the control group over the treatment group, the difference was not statistically significant. Specifically, analysis of variance results were:

- *Letter identification.* A two-way analysis of variance indicated that the advantage for the OSEO groups over the INA group was statistically significant, $F(1,241) = 10.19$, $p < .01$. The effect for treatment group was also significant, $F(3,241) = 4.21$, $p < .01$. The interaction between sponsor and treatment was not significant, $F(3,241) = 2.35$, N.S.
- *Syllable identification.* A two-way analysis of variance indicated that there was a statistically significant effect of sponsor, $F(1,229) = 32.63$, $p < .01$, and treatment type, $F(3, 229) = 4.66$, $p < .01$. The interaction between sponsor and treatment type was also significant, $F(3, 229) = 3.85$, $p < .05$.
- *Word identification.* The two-way analysis of variance for the word identification test indicated that sponsor was a significant source of variance, $F(1,207) = 24.89$, $p < .01$. Treatment condition was also a significant source of variance, $F(3, 207) = 5.99$, $p < .01$. The phonological awareness treatment group in INA classrooms did not complete the word identification test because the test was too difficult for them. The test of the interaction is uninterpretable given the lack of data for the phonological awareness INA group.
- *Sentence identification.* The statistical analysis for the sentence identification and understanding test was conducted only on the OSEO treatments. This analysis indicated that treatment group was not a significant source of variance, $F(3,188) = 2.66$, $p < .05$. The reader will note that all three of the treatment groups outperformed the control group on the sentence understanding test. Post hoc contrasts indicated that

the rapid reading group and the PA + RR group performed significantly better that did the control group.

The impact of the treatment conditions differed according to the agency sponsoring the courses. Learners enrolled in government courses tended to benefit most from phonological awareness training, whereas learners enrolled in OSEO courses tended to benefit most from rapid reading or the combination training. The probable reason for this differential impact is that phonological awareness training is most likely to be useful early in instruction, whereas rapid reading training is most likely to be beneficial *after* some skill in phonological awareness has been acquired. The shorter government-sponsored training allowed the benefits of phonological awareness to be felt before the benefits of rapid training became evident. In contrast, the longer OESO courses, brought out the benefits of rapid reading training.

*There were gender differences in performance.* Males tended to perform better than females in the tests. However, there was no evidence that the different treatments affected the performance of the two sexes differently.

As mentioned earlier, some tests could not be completed. The phonological awareness tests were computerized, and when the computers failed, they could not be scored. Also, results from the computer-based CAAS assessments were not interpretable, since they could be administered to only a small subset of the learner population; only 37 learners could be tested on a pre and post basis, and they were not randomly or evenly distributed among classes. Regression analyses were carried out, but the error variance due to the CAAS problems was large, and outcomes were confusing.

Differences may be statistically significant, but how practically useful are they in determining whether literacy courses should include phonological awareness and rapid reading? Educational research often uses *effect size*, a measure of the differences between treatment and control groups in standard deviation (z score) units.[3] Most effect sizes (Figure A1) are moderate to large.[4]

## Questionnaire Results

The data from the questionnaire provided a portrait of the population enrolling in the literacy programs. Some of the pertinent findings follow.

*Few questionnaire variables showed significant relationships with reading scores.* The only learner characteristics significantly related to performance on the paper-and-pencil test were the number of years of prior schooling and the age at which some learners attended Koranic school;

### Figure A1. Effect Sizes of Various Treatment Combinations

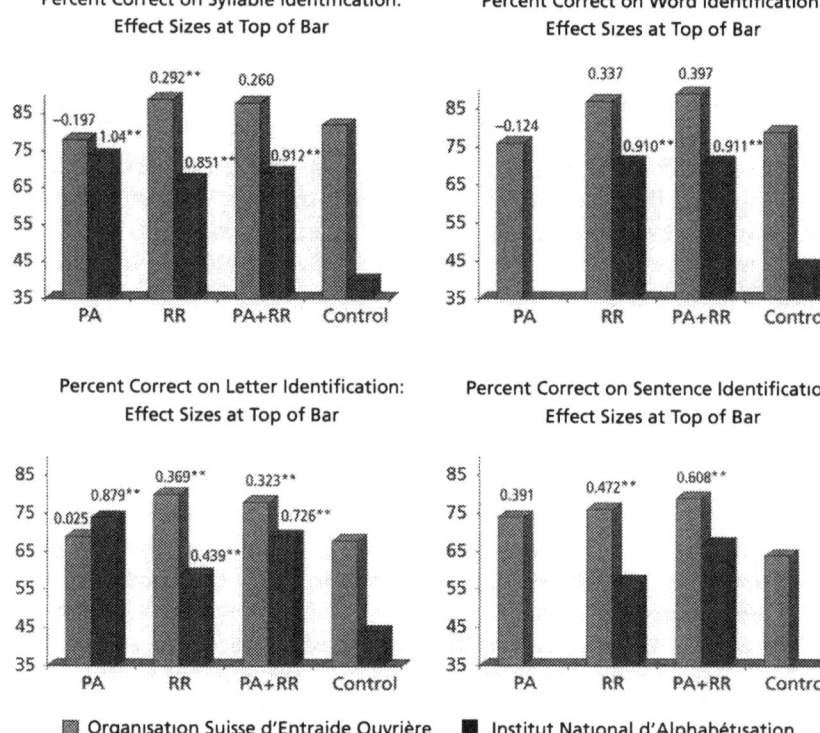

*Notes:*
** at 0.05
PA = phonological awareness; RR = rapid reading.
*Source:* Royer, Abadzi, and Kinda 2003.

those who had attended Koranic schools had better performance if they had attended at a younger age. However, only 6 percent of the learners had attended Koranic schools, and the correlation should be interpreted with caution.

*There was no relationship between self-ratings of learners and reading scores.* There was also no relationship between learners' evaluation of their own reading skills, reported reading frequency, and reading performance on the paper-and-pencil tests. It would have been expected for literates to have some insight about how well they were reading. This lack of relationship calls into question the validity of self-ratings of competence among literacy programs that use them, such as REFLECT. Similarly, a sample of learners tested in Bangladesh after course completion showed

92 percent pass, but a later retest showed only 32.3 percent of learners passing. Nevertheless, a tracer study of the same population using self-reports found that 85 percent of participants still wrote from time to time and 97 percent still read two years after program completion.[5]

It was noted that learners who had attended the rapid reading courses tended to rate themselves as better readers. It is possible that the lively reading activities promoted by this method created in the minds of the participants illusions of competence or comprehension, which are known to happen when learners are exposed to dynamic teachers and challenging learning events.[6]

About 135 graduates were interviewed and retested in May 2002, but time and funding did not permit reliable research. Most had not had anything to read for the previous year. Several had forgotten individual consonants and could read with difficulty. They did remember numbers and still could do phonological awareness exercises. Many expressed pleasure at the rapid reading and phonological exercises and some went again to the literacy class hoping that the new methods would be again applied. Given the informal observation conditions, it was not possible to estimate the incidence of relapse into illiteracy. Due to the short duration of the classes (3-4 months) learners apparently did not receive sufficient practice to consolidate skills for the long term.

## Discussion

The findings indicate that even with the short literacy class duration and the various test administration problems in the field, effects could be discerned for both cognitive methods that were tried out. The alternative hypotheses that these two methods improve reading scores above those of control classes using the "traditional" method were accepted. The research team recommended to the National Literacy Institute that these methods be adopted, and teacher training videotapes were made available to the agency.

Nevertheless, this research has been preliminary. The results of the reported research are best viewed as a pilot effort that demonstrates the potential benefit of weaving aspects of modern reading instruction into the fabric of traditional adult literacy training in developing countries. The treatments evaluated in the project were mostly "add-ons" to traditional procedures rather than tightly integrated instructional methods. Even so, the learners receiving the supplemented instruction outperformed their control school counterparts.

Possibly some of the effects of rapid reading may be due to the increased engagement and time on task that this method requires. Instead of learners watching others read inactively, they were engaged in reading with their partners much of the time. If new methods were coupled with increased time on task, literacy outcomes might be even more beneficial. Future research should evaluate this expectation. Future research should also move beyond techniques targeted solely at low-level reading skills. It should evaluate reading comprehension methods that have proved effective in developed countries. Instruction that moves from phonological awareness training, to rapid processing of syllables, words, and sentences, and then to activities designed to foster reading comprehension skill would be particularly beneficial to adults. These techniques could be integrated into existing instructional methods, thereby maintaining the cultural relevance of the instructional procedures.

To recommend that these methods become a routine part of literacy courses in other countries, more trials must be carried out in environments different from those of rural Burkina Faso. Issues to study further in future research and tryouts might be:

- A brief neuropsychological assessment should be carried out before and after the teaching program (digit span, verbal memory, working memory conceptual knowledge, visuospatial abilities), as shown by the Mexican Neuroalfa literacy program. Thus, it would be possible to find out the extent to which the cognitive processes of the graduates have improved.
- The phonological awareness exercises should be more extensive and gradually increase in complexity. They could include syllable matching and rhyme comparisons with words and non-words. It is also important to do pair discriminations and manipulate the phonemic distance between the consonants and the vowels.
- Improvements must be made in the low-level reading task logistics. The reading pack always contained the same words, so even with shuffle, learners might have memorized the range of words contained therein, since there were only 20, and these were sounded out as a reader and as a reader-timer. Perhaps longer packs should be tried.
- The amount of practice needed for the sound-letter linkages to stabilize in the memory of neoliterates must be assessed. Clearly, 3- and 4-month courses are too short for rural populations with limited daily exposure to print.

With literacy software available to supplement the fast reading tasks, an experimental use of computers could be applied in various centers. Reaction time data could be collected. Additional software, if it becomes available, could offer practice in visual scanning tasks, discrimination tasks, reading, and lexical decision tasks. Data would give information about learning process and development of automaticity. Neoliterate adults may achieve automatic reading only after a very large number of pairings of visual and auditory stimuli. Such a large number of trials is not feasible in classes, but it is feasible through computers.

## Notes

1. UNESCO Statistical Yearbook 1999–2000.

2. Easton 1998.

3. An effect size is the mean of the treatment group minus the mean of the control group divided by the standard deviation of the control group. Effect sizes may show how the average treatment group student would score *if* the students were in the control group. Sizes of 0.4–0.6 are considered small, 0.6–0.8 moderate, and above 0.8 large. For example, an effect size of 0.5, located at a statistical table of cumulative normal probabilities (area of the normal curve encompassed by various z score values), would be found to encompasses 69 percent of the normal distribution; hence the average treatment group student would score at the 69th percentile *if* they were in the control group. An effect size of 1.5 means that the average student in the treatment group would score at the 93rd percentile of the control group.

4. More detail on outcomes is provided in Abadzi 2003b.

5. Ahmad and Lohani 2001.

6. Bjork 1994, 1999.

# Appendix
# Literacy Tests and Questionnaire

The development of assessment procedures occurred in workshop during Dr. Royer's January 2001 visit to Burkina Faso. Because CAAS assessments were time-consuming and dependent on technology, an additional paper-and-pencil measure was developed that could be group-administered. All of the assessment instruments were developed in Mooré. The instruments and their contents were:

- *Phonological awareness.* The test was administered by having the examiner read two words. In some cases the learner was asked to circle yes if the words rhymed and no if they did not. Other variations of the test were circling yes if the words started with the same sound and no if they did not, or to circle yes if the words ended with the same sound, and no if they did not.
- *Letter recognition.* This test was administered by having the examiner read a letter name. The learner then selected one of four letters on the test page and circled it as the correct answer. The learner was asked to identify 20 letters.
- *Syllable recognition.* This test was administered by having the examiner read a syllable and the learner then selected one of four syllables on the test page and circled it as the correct answer. The learner was asked to identify 20 syllables.
- *Word recognition.* This test was administered by having the examiner read a word and the learner then selected one of four words on the test page and circled it as the correct answer. The learner was asked to identify 20 words.
- *Sentence recognition.* This test was administered by having the examiner read a sentence and the learner then selected one of four sentences on the test page and circled it as the correct answer. The learner was asked to identify 20 sentences.

## Learner Questionnaire

A variety of factors in addition to instructional effectiveness could influence the amount of skill acquired in adult literacy training, and the questionnaire identified some of the possible factors. The questionnaires were read to individual learners in Mooré, and the examiners coded the answers given by the learners. The following information was requested:

- The learner's gender
- The learner's age
- Whether the learner was single or married
- The number of children the learner had
- The learner's native language
- The language of reading instruction
- The number of years of previous schooling the learner had received
- Whether or not the learner attended formal school
- The age of the learner when he/she first attended formal school
- The number of years the learner attended formal school
- The level of instruction previously completed by the learner
- The number of years since the learner had attended formal school
- Whether or not the learner attended Koranic school
- The age of the learner when he/she attended Koranic school
- Whether or not the learner attended any other type of school, and if so, what kind
- The learner's evaluation of their own reading skills (e.g., very good = 1, good = 2, fair = 3, poor = 4, none = 5)
- The number of days during the academic period that the learner was absent
- The learner's motivation for learning to read
- The learner's intended use for literacy skills
- How often does the learner read (coded with 1 the most frequent)
- What does the learner read
- How many days during the instructional period that the instructor was absent

# References

Abadzi, Helen. 1994. *What We Know about Acquisition of Adult Literacy: Is there Hope?* Discussion Paper no. 245. Washington, D.C.: World Bank.
———. 1996. "Does Age Diminish the Ability to Learn Fluent Reading?" *Educational Psychology Review* 8:373–396.
———. 2003a. *Adult Literacy: A Review of Implementation Experience.* Operations Evaluation Department. Washington, D.C.: World Bank (forthcoming).
———. 2003b. "Teaching Adults to Read Better and Faster: Results from an Experiment in Burkina Faso." Policy Research Working Paper Series. Washington, D.C.: World Bank.
ActionAid International. 2001. Final Documentation and Evaluation Material from the *Comparative Action Research and Scale Up of REFLECT.* Final Report. July 25. Development Grants Facility. Washington, D.C.: World Bank.
Aftab, Tahera. 1994. "Fighting Illiteracy: What Works and What Doesn't: A Case Study of Female Literacy in Pakistan." *Convergence* 27:25–34.
Ahmed, Manzoor, and Shiv Lohani. 2001. *NFE in Bangladesh: Synthesis of Experience and Future Directions.* Dhaka: Directorate of Nonformal Education.
American Optometric Association. 1992. *Report of the AOA Task Force on Optometric Manpower.* St. Louis, MO.
Archer, David, and Sarah Cottingham. 1996. Consolidation Research Report on REFLECT: Regenerated Freirean Literacy Through Empowering Community Techniques. The Experiences of Three REFLECT Pilot Projects in Uganda, Bangladesh, and El Salvador. Official Development Assistance (ODA) Education Research Series, No. 17. World Bank.
———. 1996. *Action Research Report on REFLECT.* London: Overseas Development Administration.

Ardila, A., F. Ostrosky-Solis, and F. Mendonza, V.U. 2000a. "Learning to Read is Much More Than Learning to Read: A Neuropsychologically Based Reading Program." *Journal of the International Neuropsychological Society* 6:789–801.

Ardila, A., F. Ostrosky-Solis, M. Rosselli, and C. Gómez. 2000b. "Age Related Cognitive Decline During Normal Aging: The Complex Effect of Education." *Archives of Clinical Neuropsychology* 15:495–514.

Ardila, A., M. Rosselli, and P. Rosas. 1989. "Neuropsychological Assessment in Illiterates: Visuospatial and Memory Abilities." *Brain and Cognition* 11:147–66.

Ayari, Salah. 1995. "Diglossia and Illiteracy in the Arab World." *Language, Culture, and Curriculum* 9:243–253.

Baddeley, Alan. 1999. *Essentials of Human Memory.* East Sussex, UK: Psychology Press.

Barr, R., C. Blachowicz, C. Katz, and B. Kaufman. 2002. *Reading Diagnosis for Teachers: An Instructional Approach* (4th ed.). Boston, MA: Allyn and Bacon.

Begley, Sharon. 2000. "Mind Expansion: Inside the Teenage Brain." *Newsweek*, May 8.

Bennett, Nicholas. 1995. "Draft Preliminary Analysis of the World Bank and Adult Literacy." Washington, D.C.: World Bank (processed).

Berkman, D.S., G. Andres, R.H. Lescano, S.L. Gilman, M. Lopez, and M. M. Black. 2002. "Effects of Stunting, Diarrhoeal Disease, and Parasitic Infection during Infancy on Cognition in Late Childhood: A Follow Up Study." *The Lancet*, February 16. (Johns Hopkins University Bloomberg School Of Public Health: http://www.jhsph.edu).

Bertelson, P., B. De Gelder, L.V. Tfouni, and J. Morais. 1989. "Metaphonological Abilities of Adult Illiterates: New Evidence of Heterogeneity." *European Journal of Cognitive Psychology* 3: 239–50.

Betts, Emmet. 1964. *Foundations of Reading Instruction.* New York: American Book Co.

Bhola, H.S. 1994. *A Sourcebook for Literacy Work. Perspective for the Grassroots.* Jessica Kingsley publishers, UNESCO Publishing.

Biederman, I. 1987. " Recognition by Components: A Theory of Human Image Understanding." *Psychological Review* 94(2):115–147.

Bortfeld, Heather, and Grover J. Whitehust. 2001. "Sensitive Periods in First Language Acquisition." In D.B. Bailey, J.T. Bruer, F.J. Symons, and J.W. Lichtman (eds.), *Critical Thinking about Critical Periods.* Baltimore, MD: Paul H. Brookes Publishing Co.

Bjork, R A., and E.L. Bjork. 1992. "A New Theory of Disuse and an Old Theory of Stimulus Fluctuation." In A. Healey, S. Kosslyn, and R. Shiffrin (eds.), *From Learning Processes to Cognitive Processes: Essays in Honor of William K. Estes.* Vol. 2, p. 35–67. Hillsdale, NJ: Erlbaum.

Bjork, R.A. 1994. "Memory and Metamemory Considerations in the Training of Human Beings." In J. Metcalfe and A. Shimamura (eds.), *Metacognition: Knowing about Knowing* (p.185–205). Cambridge, MA: MIT Press.

———. 1999. "Assessing Our Own Competence: Heuristics and Illusions." In D. Gopher and A. Koriat (eds.), *Attention and Performance XVII. Cognitive Regulation of Performance: Interaction of Theory and Application* (p. 435–459). Cambridge, MA: MIT Press.

Bruner, J.S., and B.M. Bruner. 1968. "On Voluntary Action and its Hierarchical Structure. *International Journal of Psychology* 3:239–255.

Burchfield, S.A. 1997. An Analysis of the Impact of Literacy on Women's Empowerment in Nepal. *ABEL Monograph Series*, Washington D.C.: Academy for Educational Development.

Canieso Doronila, Maria Luisa 1996. "*Landscapes of Literacy: An Ethnographic Study of Functional Literacy in Marginal Philippine Communities.*" UNESCO Institute of Education.

Carr-Hill, Roy, Aikel Kweka, Mary Rusimbi, and Rustica Chendgelele. 1991. *The Functioning and Effects of the Tanzanian Literacy Programme.* UNESCO, IIEP Research Report no. 93. Paris: International Institute of Educational Planning.

Carron, Gabriel, Kilemi Mwiria, and Gabriel Righa. 1989. *The Functioning and Effects of the Kenya Literacy Programme.* Paris: International Institute of Educational Planning, UNESCO. IIEP Research Report No. 76.

Castro-Caldas A, K.M. Petersson, A. Reis, et al. 1998. "The Illiterate Brain: Learning to Read and Write During Childhood Influences the Functional Organization of the Adult Brain." *Brain* 121:1053–1063.

Cawthera, Andrew. 1999. *"Let's Teach Ourselves": A People's Literacy Movement in Bangladesh.* Manchester Monographs, Centre for Adult and Higher Education. England: University of Manchester.

———. 2001. "Nijera Shikhi, and Adult Literacy. Impact on Learners After Five Years. Effectiveness When Operating as An NGO." Eldis Development Gateway (www.eldis.org). February. Unpublished Report.

Chall, J. 1983. *Stages of Reading Development.* New York: McGraw-Hill.

Cobb, B.B, C.D. Lay, and N.M. Bourdet. 1971. *The Relationship Between Chronological Age and Aptitude Test Measures of Advanced-Level Air Traffic Control Trainees* (FAA-AM-71-36). Oklahoma City, OK: Federal Aviation Administration.

Cole, M., and B. Means. 1981. *Comparative Studies of How People Think.* Cambridge, MA: Harvard University Press.

Coltheart, M. 1978. "Lexical Access in Simple Reading Tasks." In Underwood (ed.), *Strategies of Information Processing.* London: Academic Press, p. 151–216.

Comings, John. 1995. "Literacy Skill Retention in Adult Students in Developing Countries." *International Journal of Educational Development* 15(1):37–45.

Comings, John, C.K. Shrestha, and Christine Smith. 1992. "A Secondary Analysis of a Nepalese National Literacy Program." *Comparative Education Review* 36:212–226.

Comings, J.P., C.A. Smith, S. LeVine, A.J. Dowd, and B. Garner. 1998. *A Comparison of Impact From Schooling and Participation in Adult Literacy Programs Among Women in Nepal.* Boston: World Education.

Comings, J.P., C.A. Smith, and C.K. Shrestha. (Undated). "Adult Literacy Programs: Design, Implementation and Evaluation." Boston: World Education.

Coppens, P., M.A. Parente, and A.R. Lecours. 1998. "Aphasia in Illiterate Individuals." In Patrick Coppens and Yvan Lebrun, and Anna Basso (eds.), *Aphasia in Atypical Populations.* New York: Lawrence Erlbaum Associates.

Couvert, Roger. 1979. Evaluation of Literacy Programmes. Paris: UNESCO

Delaney-Black, Virginia, Chandice Covington, Steven J. Ondersma, et al. 2002. "Violence Exposure, Trauma, and IQ and/or Reading Deficits Among Urban Children." *Archives of Pediatrics and Adolescent Medicine* 156:280–285. (reutershealth.com, March 12, 2002). http://archpedi.ama-assn.org/issues/v156n3/abs/poa10277.html

Dexter, E.R., S.E. LeVine, and P.M. Velasco. 1998. "Maternal Schooling and Health—Related Language and Literacy Skills in Rural Mexico." *Comparative Education Review* 42:139–162.

Diagne, Amadou Wade. 2001. *Programme de Formation Sur La Stratégie du 'Faire Faire' en Education des Adultes.* Dakar: Ministry of Literacy, May 7–July 5.

Diagne, Mactar. 1999. "Basic Education and Livelihood Opportunities for Illiterate and Semiliterate Young Adults—BELOISYA—Especially Young Women in Countries with Low Rates of Enrollment in Primary Schools." *Synthesis of Project Evaluation Reviews.* Human Development, Africa Region. Paper Prepared for the Review and Design Workshop. March 15–19. N'Djamena, Chad: World Bank.

Diamond, M.C., A.B. Scheibel, and L.M. Elson. 1985. *The Human Brain Coloring Book.* Oakville, C.A.: Harper Perennial.

Durgunoglu, A.Y., and B. Oney. 1999. "A Cross-Linguistic Comparison of Phonological Awareness and Word Recognition." *Reading & Writing* 11:281–299.

Easton, Peter. 1998. *Decentralization and Local Capacity Building in the Sahel: Results of the PADLOS Study.* OECD/CILSS/Club du Sahel.

Eisemon, Thomas. (Undated). "Strengthening Investments in Adult Literacy." Washington, D.C.: World Bank (processed).

Eisemon, Thomas Owen, Kari Marble, and Michael Crawford. 1995. *Investing in Adult Literacy: Lessons and Implications.* Human Development Department. Washington, D.C.: World Bank.

———. 1999. "Investing in Adult Literacy: Lessons and Implications." In Daniel Boulder, A. Wagner, Richard L. Venezky, and Brian V. Street (eds.), *Literacy. An International Handbook.* Westview Press, p. 360–366.

Elio, R., and J.R. Anderson. 1981. "The Effects of Category Generalization and Instance Similarity on Schema Abstraction." *Journal of Experimental Psychology: Human Learning and Memory* 7:397–417.

Eritrea Ministry of Education. 2002. *Eritrea National Reading Survey.* Asmara (unpublished report).

External Evaluation Team. 1993. "The Final Evaluation of the Total Literacy Campaign of Ajmer District." A report conducted by the external evaluation team (processed).

Fisk, A.D., N.D. McGee, and L.M. Giambra. 1988. "Age-Related Effects on Consistent and Varied Semantic Category Search Performance." *Psychology and Aging* 3:323–33.

Fisk, A.D., W.A. Rogers, and L.M. Giambra. 1990. "Consistent and Varied Memory/Visual Search: Is There an Interaction Between Age and Response-Set Effects?" *Journal of Gerontology: Psychological Sciences* 45:81–7.

Fisk, A.D., and W.A. Rogers. 1991. "Toward an Understanding of Age–Related Memory and Visual Search Effects". *Journal of Experimental Psychology: General* 120:131–49.

Flowers, F., T.A. Zeffiro, K. Jones, K. Cappell, L. Gareau, N. Dietz, J. Agnew, J. VanMeter, B.F. Wood, and G.F. Eden. 2001. "Functional Neuroanatomy of Reading Remediation in Dyslexia." Cognitive Neuroscience Society.

Friedman, R.B., and M.P. Alexander. 1984. "Pictures, Images, and Pure Alexia: A Case Study." *Cognitive Neuropsychology* 1:9–23.

Fujisawa, Miki. 2001. "Rural Women's Perspectives on Adult Literacy Education and Development in Kenya." Presented at the Annual Conference of the Comparative and International Education Society. March 14–17. Washington, D.C.

Gaillard, W.D., L.M. Balsamo, Z. Ibrahim, B.C. Sachs, and B. Xu. 2003. "fMRI Identifies Regional Specialization of Neural Networks for Reading in Young Children." *Neurology* 60:94–100.

Gathercole, S., and A. Baddeley. 1993. *Working Memory and Language.* Hove, UK: Lawrence Erlbaum.

Gay, J., and M. Cole. 1967. *The New Mathematics and an Old Culture: A Study of Learning Among the Kpelle of Liberia*. New York: Holt, Rinehardt, and Winston.

Gray, Scott William. 1953. *Preliminary Survey on Methods of Teaching Reading and Writing*. Paris: UNESCO.

Gibson, E.J., and H. Levin. 1975. *The Psychology of Reading*. Cambridge, MA: MIT Press

Gibson, E.J., and A.D. Pick. 2000. *An Ecological Approach to Perceptual Learning and Development*. Oxford and New York: Oxford University Press.

Gibson, E.J., A. Pick, H. Osser., and M. Hammond. 1962. "The Role of Grapheme-Phoneme Correspondence in the Perception of Words." *American Journal of Psychology* 75:554–570.

Gillund, G., and R.M. Shiffrin. 1984. "A Retrieval Model for Both Recognition and Recall." *Psychological Review* 91:1–67.

Godwin, Peter. 2001. "Bushmen: Southern Africa's Hunter-Gatherers Seek a Foothold." *National Geographic* 1999:90–117.

Goldstone, R.L. 1998. "Perceptual Learning." *Annual Review of Psychology* 49:585–612.

Goldstone, R.L, Y. Lippa, and R.M. Shiffrin. 2001. "Altering Object Representations through Category Learning." *Cognition* 78:27–43.

Gombert, J.E. 1994. "How Do Illiterate Adults React to Metalinguistic Training?" *Annals of Dyslexia* 44:250–269.

Greenberg, Daphne, L. Ehri, and D. Perin. 1997. "Are Word-Reading Processes the Same or Different in Adult Literacy Students and Third–Fifth Graders Matched for Reading Level?" *Journal of Educational Psychology* 89:262–75.

Greenfield, Patricia. 1991. "Language, Tools and the Brain: The Ontogeny and Phylogeny of Hierarchically Organized Sequential Behavior." *Behavioral and Brain Sciences* 14:531–595.

Haddad, Wadi. 1994. *The Dynamics of Education Policymaking*. Economic Development Institute. Analytical Case Studies No. 10. Washington, D.C.: World Bank.

Hamadache, Ali, and Daniel Martin. 1986. *Theory and Practice of Literacy Work*. Paris: UNESCO.

Hanley, J. Richard, O. Tzeng, and H.S. Huang. 1999. "Learning to Read Chinese." In M. Harris and G. Hatano (eds.), *Learning to Read and Write: A Cross-Linguistic Perspective*. Cambridge, UK: Cambridge University Press.

Harris, Margaret, and Giyoo Hatano. 1999. "Introduction: A Cross-Linguistic Perspective on Learning to Read and Write." In M. Harris and G. Hatano (eds), *Learning to Read and Write: A Cross-Linguistic Perspective*. Cambridge, UK: Cambridge University Press.

Harris, William. 1989. *Ancient Literacy*. Cambridge, MA: Harvard University Press.
Hashemi, Syed, Sidney Schuler, and Ann Riley. 1996. "Rural Credit Programs and Women's Empowerment in Bangladesh." *World Development* 24(4):635–653.
Henderson, V.W., R.B. Friedman, E.L. Teng, and J.M. Weiner. 1985. "Left Hemisphere Pathways in Reading: Inferences From Pure Alexia Without Hemianopia." *Neurology* 35(7):962–968.
Hintzman, D.L. 1986. "Schema Abstraction in a Multiple Trace Model." *Psychological Review* 93:411–428.
Instituto Nacional de Educación para los Adultos. 1998. "Prueba Diagnóstica de Alfabetización." *Manuales de Evaluación de la Dirección de Contenidos* (Diagnostic Test of Learning to Read Manuals from the Content Directorate). México, DF. México: INEA.
Iredale, R. 1994. "Why Do Donors Find Literacy Difficult?" *Journal of Practice in Education for Development* 1:31–33.
Jacoby, L.L., R.A. Bjork, and C.M. Kelley. 1994. "Illusions of Comprehensions and Competence." In D. Druckman and R.A. Bjork (eds.), *Learning, Remembering, Believing: Enhancing Human Performance* (pp. 57–80). Washington, D.C.: National Academy Press
Jejeebhoy, S. 1996. *Women's Education, Autonomy, and Reproductive Behavior: Experience from Developing Countries*. Oxford: Clarendon Press.
Jennings, J. 1990. *Adult Literacy: Master or Servant?* Dhaka: University Press Ltd.
Jones, Phillip W. 1988. *International Policies for Third World Education*: UNESCO: Literacy and Development (Routhledge).
———. 1990. "Literacy and Basic Education for Adults and Young People: Review of Experience." A Special Study for the World Conference on Education for All. Paris: UNESCO.
———. 1997. "The World Bank and the Literacy Question: Orthodoxy, Heresy, and Ideology." *International Review of Education* 43:367–375.
Kanizsa, Gaetano. 1979. *Organization in Vision: Essays on Gestalt Perception*. New York: Praeger.
Karlekar, Malavika. 2000. *Reading the World: Understanding the Literacy Campaign in India*. Mumbai: Asian South Pacific Bureau of Adult Education.
King, Kenneth. 1978. *Literacy In Developing Countries*. Ottawa: International Development Research Center.
Korboe, David. 1997. *Ghana: Literacy and Functional Skills Project (Cr. 2349-GH). Beneficiary Impact Assessment*. Accra: Ministry of Education and IDA.
Kujala, Teija, et al. 2001. "Audiovisual Training Helps Children with Dyslexia." Proceedings of the National Academy of Sciences 98:10509–10514 (www.reutershealth.com), August 20.

Laboratory of Comparative Human Cognition. 1986. "Contribution of Cross-Cultural Research to Educational Science." *American Psychologist* 41:1049–58.

Lauglo, John. 2001. *Engaging with Adults: The Case for Increased Support to Adult Basic Education in Sub-Saharan Africa.* Africa Region. February. Washington, D.C.: World Bank.

Lecours, A.R. 1989. "Literacy and Acquired Aphasia." In A.M. Galaburda (ed.), *From Reading to Neurons.* Cambridge, MA: MIT Press.

Lennenberg, E. 1967. *Biological Foundations of Language.* New York: Wiley.

Levi, Don. 1996. "Why Do Illiterates Do So Badly in Logic?" *Philosophical Investigation* 19:35–54.

LeVine R., S. LeVine, and B. Schnell. 2001. "Improve the Women: Mass Schooling, Female Literacy and Worldwide Social Change." Harvard Educational. *Harvard Educational Review* 71(1):1–50.

Levinger, B. 1992. *Nutrition, Health, and Learning.* School Nutrition and Health Network Monograph Series 1. Newton, MA: Education Development Center.

Limage, Leslie. 1999. "Comparative Perspectives on Language and Literacy." Selected papers from the work of the Language and Literacy Commission of the 10th World Progress of Comparative Education Societies in Cape Town (1998). Dakar: UNESCO Regional Office.

Lind, Agneta. 1996. *Free to Speak Up: Overall Evaluation of the National Literacy Programme In Namibia.* Directorate of Adult Basic Education, Ministry of Basic Education and Culture, Windhoek.

———. 1997. "Adult Literacy in the Third World—A Review of Trends a Decade Later." *NORRAG NEWS* 21:31–35.

Lind, Agneta, and Anton Johnston 1990. *Adult Literacy in the Third World. A Review of Objectives and Strategies.* Stockholm: SIDA.

Logan, G.D., and S.T. Klapp. 1991. "Automatizing Alphabetic Arithmetic: Evidence for an Instance Theory of Automatization." *Journal of Experimental Psychology,* 17(2): 179–195.

Logan, G.D., S.E. Taylor, and J.L. Etherton. 1996. "Attention in the Acquisition and Expression of Automaticity." *Journal of Experimental Psychology: Learning, Memory and Cognition* 22(3):620–638.

Lott, S.N., and R.B. Friedman. 1999. "Can Treatment for Pure Alexia Improve Letter-By-Letter Reading Speed Without Sacrificing Accuracy?" *Brain and Language* 67:188–201.

Lott, S.N., R.B. Friedman, and C.W. Linebaugh. 1994. "Rationale and Efficacy of a Tactile-Kinaesthetic Treatment for Alexia." *Aphasiology* 8:181–195.

Lowe, David. 1985. *Perceptual Organization and Visual Recognition.* Boston: Kluwer Academic Publishers.

Lukatela, Katerina, Claudia Carello, Donald Shankweiler, and Ilabelle Liberman. 1995. "Phonological Awareness in Illiterates: Observations From Serbo-Croatian." *Applied Psycholinguistics* 16:463–487.
Mace, J. 1999. Women's Education Programme, Gedaref, Sudan. An Evaluation of a WUS (UK) Project, London: World University Service.
Madden, D.J., and R.D. Nebes. 1980. "Aging and the Development of Automaticity in Visual Search." *Developmental Psychology* 16:377–84.
Madden, D.J. 1983. "Aging and Distraction by Highly Familiar Stimuli During Visual Search." *Developmental Psychology* 19:499–507.
McAuliffe, J.F., and L. Falsao. 1993. "Understanding of Growth Monitoring Charts by Literate and Illiterate Mothers in Northeast Brazil." *Journal of Tropical Pediatrics* 39:370–393.
McKenna, S.P., and A.I. Glendon. 1985. "Occupational First Aid Training: Decay in CPR Skills." *Journal of Occupational Psychology* 58:109–117.
Maguire, E.A., R.S. Frackowiak, and C.D. Frith. 1997. "Recalling Routes around London: Activation of the Right Hippocampus in Taxi Drivers. *Journal of Neuroscience* 17(18):7103–10.
Merzenich, William Jenkins, Paul Johnston, Christoph Schreiner, Steve Miller, and Paula Tallal. 1996. "Temporal Processing Deficits of Language-Learning Impaired Children Ameliorated by Training." *Science* 271:77–81.
Morais, José, L.J. Alegría, L. Cary, and P. Bertelson. 1979. "Does Awareness of Speech as a Sequence of Phones Arise Spontaneously?" *Cognition* 7:323–331.
Morais, José, Sao Luis Castro, Leonor Scliar-Cabral, Regine Kolinsky, and Alain Content. 1987. "Effects of Literacy on the Recognition of Dichotic Words." *The Quarterly Journals of Experimental Psychology* 39A: 451–465.
Morais, José, Alain Content, Paul Bertelson, Luz Cary, and Regine Kolinsky. 1988. "Is There a Critical Period for the Acquisition of Segmental Analysis?" *Cognitive Neuropsychology* 5(3):347–352.
Moulton, Jeanne. 1997. *Non-formal Education and Empowered Behavior.* Washington, D.C.: Academy for Educational Development.
———. 2001. *Improving Education in Rural Areas: Guidance for Rural Development Specialists.* Washington, D.C.: World Bank.
National Reading Panel. 2000. *Teaching Children to Read.* Institute of Child Health, National Institutes of Health. Available at (www.nationalreadingpanel.org).
Neergard, Lauran. 2001. "Computerized Educational Games Help Kids Overcome Learning Disabilities." (Nandonet.com/healthscience). October 15. Washington, D.C.: Associated Press.
Neisser, Ulrich. 1964. "Visual Search." *Scientific American* 210(6):94–102.

New Era. 1989. *Evaluation Study of Literacy Campaign in Surkhet Valley.* Kathmandu, Nepal (processed).

———. 1990. *Evaluation Study of Literacy Programme of SFDP and PCRW.* Kathmandu, Nepal (processed).

Okech, Anthony, Roy Carr-Hill, Ann Katahoire, et al. 1999. *Report of Evaluation of the Functional Adult Literacy Programme in Uganda.* Kampala: Ministry of Gender, Labour and Social Development.

Okech, A., R. Carr-Hill, A. Katahoire, T. Kakooza, A.N. Ndidde, and J. Oxenham (Evaluation Team). 2001. *Adult Literacy Programs in Uganda.* Africa Region Human Development Series. Washington, D.C.: World Bank.

Ostrosky, F., A. Ardila, M. Rosselli, G. López-Arango, and V. Uriel-Mendoza. 1998. "Neuropsychological Test Performance in Illiterates." *Archives of Clinical Neuropsychology* 13:645–660.

Oxenham, John, Abdoul Hamid Diallo, Anne Ruhweza Katahoire, Anna Petkova-Mwang, and Oumar Sall. 2002. "Skills and Literacy Training for Better Livelihoods." Human Development Sector, Africa Region. Washington, D.C.: World Bank.

Oxenham, John, and Aya Aoki. 2002. *Including the 900 Million.* Washington, D.C.: World Bank (draft).

Oxenham, John, and Maktar Diagne. 2001. "Synthesis of the Evaluations of 27 Programs in Adult Basic Education with Literacy and Numeracy." In John Oxenham (ed.), *Proceedings of a Workshop in Programs of Adult Basic Education and Training with Literacy and Numeracy.* Washington D.C.: World Bank and International Literacy Institute.

Oxenham, John. 2002. "Review of World Bank Supported Projects in Adult Basic Education and Literacy, 1977-2002: Comparison of Costs." World Bank: Human Development Network (Draft).

Oxenham, John. 1974. *The Turkish Project in Functional Education for Family Life Planning.* Cambridge, MA: Harvard University Graduate School of Education.

Patel, S., B. Balate, F. Tembe, M. Bazima, G. Macabi, and M. Sánchez. 2000. *Evaluation Report of Adult and Non-Formal Education Programs in Mozambique.* Republic of Mozambique: Ministry of Education.

Paulesu, Eraldo, Uta Frith, Margaret Snowling, Alice Gallagher, et al. 1996. "Is Developmental Dyslexia a Disconnection Syndrome? Evidence form PET Scanning." *Brain* 119:143–157.

Paulesu, E., F. Demonet, F. Fazio, E. McCrory, et al. 2001. "Dyslexia: Cultural Diversity and Biological Unity." *Science* (GSCI) 291(n5511): 2165–2167.

Perfetto, G., D. Bransford, and J. Franks. 1983. "Constraints on Access in a Problem Solving Context." *Memory and Cognition* 11:24–31.

Petersen, S.E., P.T. Fox, A.Z. Snyder, and M.E. Raichle. 1990. "Activation of Extrastriate and Frontal Cortical Areas by Visual Words and Word-Like Stimuli." *Science* 249:1041–44.

Petersson, Karl Magnus, Alexandra Reis, and Martin Ingvar. 2001. "Cognitive Processing in Literate and Illiterate Subjects: A Review of Some Recent Behavioral and Functional Neuroimaging Data." *Scandinavian Journal of Psychology* 42:251–267.

Plude, D.J., and W.J. Hoyer. 1981. "Adult Age Differences in Visual Search as a Function of Stimulus Mapping and Processing Load." *Journal of Gerontology* 36:598–604.

Plude, D.J., D.B. Kaye, W.J. Hoyer, T.A. Post, M.J. Saynisch, and M.V. Hahn. 1983. "Aging and Visual Search Under Consistent and Varied Mapping." *Developmental Psychology* 19:508–12.

Posner, M.I., and M.E. Raichle. 1997. "Deep Dyslexia: A Case Study of Connectionist Neuropsychology." *Cognitive Neuropsychology* 10:377–500.

Rabia, S.A. 1995. "Learning to Read in Arabic: Reading Syntactic, Orthographic and Working Memory Skills in Normally Achieving and Poor Arabic Readers." *Reading Psychology* 16:351–391.

Ratcliff, R. 1978. "A Theory of Memory Retrieval." *Psychological Review* 85:59–108.

Rayner, Keith, Barbara R. Foorman, Charles A. Perfetti, David Pesetsky, and Mark S. Seidenberg. 2001. "How Psychological Science Informs the Teaching of Reading." *Psychological Science in the Public Interest* 2:1–33 (http://www.psychologicalscience.org/newsresearch/publications/journals/pspi/pspi22.pdf).

Read, C., Y.F. Zhang, H.Y. Nie, and B.Q. Ding. 1984. "The Ability to Manipulate Speech Sound Depends on Knowing Alphabetic Writing." *Cognition* 24:31–44.

Reicher, G.M. 1969. "Perceptual Recognition as a Function of the Meaningfulness of the Stimulus Material." *Journal of Experimental Psychology* 81:275–280.

Reis, Alexandra, Karl Magnus Petersson, Alexandre Castro-Caldas, and Martin Ingvar. 2001. "Formal Schooling Influences Two- but Not Three-Dimensional Naming Skills." *Brain and Cognition* 47:397–411.

Reis, Alexandra, and Alexcandre Castro Caldas. 1997. "Illiteracy: A Bias for Cognitive Development." *Journal of International Neuropsychological Society* 3:444–450.

Riddell, Abby. 2001. "A Review of 13 Evaluations of Reflect." ActionAid International. June.

Romain, R., and L. Armstrong. 1987. *Review of World Bank Operations in Non-formal Education and Training.* Education and Training Series no. 63. Washington, D.C.: World Bank.

Rogers, A. 1991. *Partners in Literacy*. Reading, UK: Education for Development.
Roy, P., and J.M. Kapoor. 1975. *The Retention of Literacy*. Delhi: MacMillan Co. of India.
Royer, J. 1997. "A Cognitive Perspective on the Assessment, Diagnosis, and Remediation of Reading Skills." In G. Phye (ed.), *Handbook of Academic Learning*. New York: Academic Press.
Royer, J.M., Abadzi, H., and Kinda, J. 2003. "The Impact of Phonological Awareness and Rapid Reading Training on the Reading Skills of Adolescent and Adult Neoliterates in Burkina Faso." *International Review of Education* (in press).
Rumsey, J.M., K. Nace, B. Donohue, D. Wise, J.M. Maisog, and P. Andreason. 1997. "A Positron Emission Tomographic Study of Impaired Word Recognition and Phonological Processing in Dyslexic Men." *Archives of Neurology* 54:562–573
Saldanha, Denzil. 2000. *The REFLECT Approach to Adult Education in India: Process and Policy Implications*. DFID-India, New Delhi Tata Institute of Social Sciences. Mumbai. May.
Saldanha, Denzil, K.S. Ahmed, A. Haq, S.D. Khan, R. Sengupta, and S.R. Uddin. 1999. *Evaluation Study of REFLECT in Bangladesh: A Participatory Collaborative Review*. Dhaka: ActionAid-Bangladesh.
Salmi, Jamil. 1987. "Language and Schooling in Morocco." *International Journal of Educational Development* 7:21–31.
Salthouse, T.A. 1991. *Theoretical Perspectives on Cognitive Aging*. Hillsdale, NJ: Lawrence Erlbaum Associates.
Salthouse, T.A., and B. Somberg. 1982. "Skilled Performance: Effects of Adult Age and Experience on Elementary Processes." *Journal of Experimental Psychology: General* 111:176–207.
Sampson, Geoffrey. 1985. *Writing Systems*. Stanford, CA: Stanford University Press.
Sanogo, M., D. Kone, and A. Konare. 1999. *Rapport d'Évaluation à Mi-Parcours du Programme de Save the Children/USA, Kolondiéba*. Kolondiéba, Mali, Save the Children.
Schneider, W. 1986. "Toward a Model of Attention and the Development of Automatic Processing." In M.I. Posner and O.S. Marin (eds.), *Attention and Performance XI*. Hillsdale, NJ: Erlbaum (p. 475–492).
Scribner, S., and M. Cole. 1978. "Unpacking Literacy." *Social Science Information* 7:19–40.
———. 1981. *The Psychology of Literacy*. Boston: Harvard University Press.
Seidenberg, M.S., and J.L. McClelland. 1989. "Visual Word Recognition and Pronunciation: A Computational Model of Acquisition, Skilled Performance, and Dyslexia." In A.M. Galaburda (ed.), *From Reading to Neurons*. Cambridge, MA: MIT Press.
Sekuler, Robert, and Randolph Blake. 2001. *Perception*. New York: McGraw-Hill.

Shaywitz, S.E., et al. 1998. "Functional Disruption in the Organization of the Brain for Reading in Dyslexia." *Proceedings of the National Academy of Sciences, USA* 95:2636–2641.

Shaywitz, Bennett A., Sally E. Shaywitz, Kenneth R. Pugh, W. Einar Mencl, et al. 2002. "Disruption of Posterior Brain Systems for Reading in Children with Developmental Dyslexia." *Biological Psychiatry* 52 (http://www-east.elsevier.com/bps/abstracts/16355abs.htm).

Shiffrin, R.M., and W. Schneider. 1977. "Controlled and Automatic Human Information Processing: II Perceptual Learning, Automatic Attending, and a General Theory." *Psychological Review* 84:127–190.

Solan, Harold, Jerome Feldman, and Laura Tujak. 1995. "Developing Visual and Reading Efficiency in Older Adults". *Optometry and Vision Science* 72:139–145.

Stanovich, Keith E. 1988. "The Right and Wrong Places to Look for the Cognitive Locus of Reading Disability." *Annals of Dyslexia* 38:154–177.

———. 1993–94. "Romance and Reality (Distinguished Educator Series)." *Reading Teacher* 47(4):280–91 (EJ 477 302).

Sticht, Thomas. 1997. *Functional Context Education: Making Learning Relevant.* Sponsored by the Applied Behavioral and Cognitive Sciences, Inc. The National Adult Literacy Database. The Centre for Literacy, Montreal and Alberta College, Calgary, Canada.

Stroop, J.R. 1935. "Studies of Interference in Serial Verbal Reactions." *Journal of Experimental Psychology* 18:643–662.

St. Sauver, Jennifer L. 2001. "Roots of Reading Problems May Differ by Sex." *American Journal of Epidemiology* 154:787–794.

Museum of the Alphabet. 1990. *The Alphabet Makers.* Waxhaw, North Carolina: Summer Institute of Linguistics.

Thomas, Wayne P., and Virginia Collier. 1997. School Effectiveness for Language Minority Students (http://www.ncbe.gwu.edu).

Torres, Rosa M. 2001. "Lifelong Learning: Where and How Does Adult Basic Education Fit." Instituto Fronesis (www.fronesis.org).

Treisman, A., and G. Gelade. 1980. "A Feature Integration Theory of Attention." *Cognitive Psychology* 12:97–136.

Trites, D.K. 1963. "Ground Support Personnel." *Aerospace Medicine* 34:539–41.

Trites, D.K., and B.B. Cobb. 1964a. "Problems in Air Traffic Management: III. Implications of Training-Entry Age for Training and Job Performance of Air Traffic Control Specialists." *Aerospace Medicine* 35:336–40.

———. 1964b. "Problems in Air Traffic Management: IV. Comparison of Pre-Employment, Job-Related Experience with Aptitude Tests as Predictors of Training and Job Performance of Air Traffic Control Specialists." *Aerospace Medicine* 35:428–36.

UNESCO. 1999–2000. *Statistical Yearbook.*
———. 2000. Education For All—The Dakar Framework for Action. Dakar, Senegal, April 26–28 (http://unesdoc.unesco.org/images/0012/001211/121147e.pdf).
UNESCO/UNDP. 1976. *The Experimental World Literacy Programme: A Critical Assessment.* Paris: UNESCO Press.
Varney, Nils R. 2002. "How Reading Works: Considerations from Prehistory to the Present." *Applied Neuropsychology* 9:3–12.
Venezky, Richard, Oney Banu, John Sabatini, and Richa Jain. 1998. "Teaching Adults to Read and Write: A Research Synthesis." Paper prepared for Abt Associates, Inc. March 1.
Venezky, Richard L. 2001. "Foundations for Studying Basic Processes in Reading." Paper prepared for the NATO Advanced Study Institute: Literacy Acquisition, Assessment, & Intervention: The Role of Phonology, Orthography, and Morphology. Il Ciocco, Tuscany, Italy, November 5–16, 2001.
Wagner, Daniel. 1995. "Literacy and Development: Rationales, Myths, Innovations, and Future Directions." *International Journal of Educational Development* 15(4):341–362.
Wheeler, D.D. 1970. "Processes in Word Recognition." *Cognitive Psychology* 1:59–85.
Wilkinson, Lucy, Andrew Scholey, and Keith Wesnes. 2002. "Chewing Gum Selectively Improves Aspects of Memory in Healthy Volunteers." *Appetite* 38:235–236.
Wisher, Robert. 1992. "The Role of Complexity on Retention of Psychomotor and Procedural Skills." Proceedings of the Human Factors Society 36th Annual Meeting.
World Bank. 1995. *Priorities and Strategies for Education.* Education Sector Human Development Network. Washington, D.C.: World Bank.
———. 2001. *Education for Dynamic Economies: Accelerating Progress Towards Education for All.* Human Development Network. Washington, D.C.: World Bank.
Zeffiro, T., and G. Eden. 2000. "The Neural Basis of Developmental Dyslexia." *Annals of Dyslexia* 50:3–30.

# Index

abstract speech, 18, 19
accuracy of reading, 2, 8, 27, 28, 31, 37, 48, 52, 77, 80, 81, 82, 84
ActionAid, 21, 25, 64, 68, 69, 92
adolescent literacy learners, 45, 56, 82
air traffic control training, 46
alexia reading disorder, 39, 48, 49
Arabic script, 6, 33, 36, 37, 38, 39, 42, 45, 48, 49, 56, 57, 58, 72, 77, 86
attendance in literacy classes, 2, 11, 64, 65, 67, 72, 81, 85, 86
attention span, 17, 20, 28
automatic reading, 1, 2, 5, 13, 29, 30, 31, 32, 36, 37, 38, 47, 50, 53, 63, 72, 75, 95
Automatic reading, 1, 2, 5, 13, 29, 30, 31, 32, 36, 37, 38, 47, 50, 53, 63, 75, 95
automaticity, 4, 7, 29, 30, 31, 41, 44, 46, 49, 52, 53, 54, 56, 58, 62, 63, 66, 75, 77, 84, 95
Bangladesh literacy programs, 9, 11, 44, 47, 61, 69, 92
Bengali script, 40, 45, 49, 52
brain as a computer, 8, 17, 28, 32, 48, 54, 66, 80, 81, 90
Brain as a computer, 8, 80
Brain imaging, 15, 29, 30, 52

Burkina Faso, 1, 11, 27, 31, 33, 45, 46, 57, 62, 65, 66, 67, 77, 79, 80, 81, 82, 85, 86, 94, 97
calculations, 7, 62, 63, 69
Cape Verde literacy programs, 61
cards for fast reading, 4
categorization skills, 18, 21
Chinese ideograms, 33, 55, 57
cognitive limitations of the unschooled, 20, 21
computer-based academic assessment system, 80, 81, 84, 85, 87, 90, 97
Computer-based Academic Assessment System (CAAS), 80, 81, 84, 85, 87, 90, 97
computers in literacy, 81
context processor, 22
cost of literacy, 12
critical periods of development, 46
Cyrillic script, 61
deciphering, 2, 9, 16, 22, 28, 32, 38, 49, 67, 69
decisionmaking process of illiterates, 17, 20, 21, 78
decoding, 7, 17, 24, 25, 26, 27, 28, 32, 33, 35, 36, 40, 42, 45, 46, 50, 57, 59, 61, 64, 77, 86
decontextualized speech, 18, 68

deductive reasoning, 18
developmental periods, 46
digits, 8, 51, 76, 94
dual route theory of memory, 55
Dutch spelling, 40
dyslexia, 15, 18, 47, 48, 59, 77, 80
empowerment, 2, 7, 11, 21, 68, 69, 70, 72, 73, 78
encapsulation of words, 29, 38
English language, 15, 26, 32, 34, 40, 47, 48, 49, 56
evaluation, 45, 62, 70, 72, 92, 98
evoked potentials, 50, 53
evolutionary origins of reading, 17
expert reading, 1, 24, 30, 34, 35, 36, 77
eye fixations, 34, 35
eye movements, 35
eye saccades, 34, 35, 77
eyesight, 6, 64
Eye-track, 55
faster reading, 95
forgetting, 5, 6, 41, 43, 44, 57, 79
French language, 26, 33, 40, 42, 45, 48, 59, 80
Functional magnetic resonance imaging, 15, 59, 77
fusiform gyrus, 55
geons, 16, 36, 55
gestalt principles, 36, 55
Ghana literacy programs, 48, 67, 68, 69
giardia, 47
group formation in literacy, 20, 67, 80
group formation, 6, 67
health issues affecting reading, 47
Hindi script, 6, 39, 41, 49, 54, 58
hippocampus, 51, 57, 59
illusions of competence, 70
income generation, 6, 67, 72
Indian scripts, 56, 61
information processing, 29, 32
Iodine deficiency, 47
Italian language, 40, 56, 57
Kenya literacy programs, 11, 48, 66

kinesthetic learning, 6, 48, 56
language and reading, 4, 12, 15, 17, 18, 19, 22, 24, 25, 26, 31, 32, 33, 42, 46, 48, 51, 54, 58, 59, 62, 63, 67, 68, 77, 80, 81, 83, 87, 97, 98
Latin script, 6, 37, 39, 40, 46, 54, 55, 58, 77
Laubach method, 25
Leapfrog computer, 5, 54
letter combinations, 4, 24, 31, 33, 36, 40, 56, 61
letter shapes, 22, 37, 43, 46
literacy course dropout, 1, 9, 11, 12, 50, 66
literacy course duration, 62, 70
literacy-second approach, 2, 67
Luria, Alexander, 17, 51
magnetic source imaging, 50
Magnetoencephalography, 50
memory, 1, 2, 3, 7, 8, 12, 17, 19, 20, 21, 25, 26, 27, 28, 29, 30, 31, 32, 33, 35, 37, 42, 43, 44, 45, 47, 48, 49, 51, 52, 53, 54, 57, 58, 59, 62, 66, 72, 75, 76, 78, 82, 83, 84, 94
mental dictionary, 22, 55
microcredit and literacy, 20
mnemonics, 4, 5, 25, 26, 44, 77
money management, 68
monitoring, 54, 66, 75
Mooré language, 45, 62, 65, 80, 81, 84, 97
Nepalese literacy programs, 69
neural networks, 3, 17, 22
Neuroalfa literacy method, 3, 20, 21, 94
neuropsychological research, 3, 12, 15, 20, 21, 51, 94
Neuropsychological tests, 3, 20, 21
Nomgana region (Burkina Faso), 67, 80, 84, 85
nonformal education, 10, 11, 13
nongovernmental organizations (NGOs), 12, 21, 69, 76, 77, 79

# Index

norms for reading achievement, 1, 27, 52, 79, 82
Norms for reading achievement, 79, 82
orthographic processor, 22, 23
overlearning reading, 31, 54
parietal lobe, 50
participatory rural appraisal, 4, 21
perceptual discrimination, 19, 37, 38, 40, 56, 59, 95
perceptual learning, 6, 25, 37, 39, 46, 48, 50, 56, 75, 77
phonographix, 4, 25, 52
phonological awareness, 7, 8, 15, 18, 21, 32, 33, 46, 54, 55, 66, 76, 81, 84, 86, 89, 90, 93, 94
phonological processor, 22, 23, 24
planum temporale, 50
Portuguese illiterates, 15, 50
Positron emission tomography, 15, 18, 50, 59
poverty alleviation, 9, 11, 20, 72, 78
pragnanz in gestalt, 35, 49
pseudowords, 4, 16, 18, 25, 50, 52
psychomotor skills, 41, 47
rapid reading, 28, 84, 89, 90, 93
reading speed, 2, 8, 25, 28, 30
reciprocal teaching, 7, 66
REFLECT literacy method, 21, 25, 64, 68, 69, 92
relapse into illiteracy, 2, 5, 27, 29, 41, 44, 70
researcher bias, 70
same-language subtitling, 4, 31
self-confidence, 68, 70, 72
self-reports, reading achievement, 2, 7, 11, 69, 70, 93
semantic processor, 22, 23, 48
Senegal literacy programs, 10, 61, 65, 66, 67

short-term memory, 1, 3, 7, 8, 20, 26, 27, 28, 29, 30, 31, 33, 42, 45, 48, 51, 52, 54, 57, 62, 66, 76, 78, 83, 84, 94
software for literacy, 17, 54, 95
speech comprehension, 2, 18, 78
speed-reading, 4, 25
strokes, 18, 36, 53
sustainability of literacy, 2, 7, 21, 72
syllabic scripts, 22, 36, 38, 39, 40, 46, 48, 49, 54, 55, 56, 61, 77
Syllabic scripts, 16, 40
syllogisms of illiterates, 18, 62
temporal lobe, 59
textbooks, 4, 6, 25, 38, 39, 43, 52, 63, 64, 69
time on task, 2, 7, 66, 86
tonal languages, 25
topological imprinting, 56
Total Literacy Campaigns, 64
tracing letters, 39
transfer of learning, 56
Uganda literacy programs, 11, 44, 48, 62, 66, 69
UNESCO, 12, 13, 28, 53, 96
unitization principle, 38, 40
verbal memory, 21, 51, 94
videotaped role modeling, 44, 66, 72, 93
visual tests, 6, 64
visuospatial abilities, 6, 19, 20, 39, 94
word superiority effect, 4, 24, 25, 52
working memory, 1, 2, 3, 7, 8, 20, 26, 27, 28, 29, 30, 31, 33, 42, 45, 47, 48, 51, 52, 54, 57, 59, 62, 66, 76, 78, 83, 84, 94
writing, 6, 17, 21, 33, 39, 41, 42, 43, 47, 51, 54, 55, 64, 84
Yugoslavia, 15

www.ingramcontent.com/pod-product-compliance
Lightning Source LLC
Chambersburg PA
CBHW032004080426
42735CB00007B/508